The Engaged Teacher

What Works with Today's Students

By Nancy Vader-McCormick

Foreword by Terry O'Banion

NEW
FORUMS

Stillwater, Oklahoma
U.S.A.

To Ralph!
A fabulous person &
amazing person &
teacher - Keep on
engaging students
Best!
Nancy

NEW FORUMS PRESS INC.

Published in the United States of America
by New Forums Press, Inc.1018 S. Lewis St.
Stillwater, OK 74074
www.newforums.com

Library of Congress Cataloging-in-Publication Data Pending

This book may be ordered in bulk quantities at discount from New
Forums Press, Inc., P.O. Box 876, Stillwater, OK 74076 [Federal I.D.
No. 73 1123239]. Printed in the United States of America.

Cover photography by Melissa Lile.

ISBN 10: 1-58107-219-8
ISBN 13: 978-1-581072-19-8

If we are serious in our efforts to enhance college success, much must change. We must focus our efforts on the classroom and reshape the work of faculty and the experience of students.

—Vince Tinto (2011)

Visit the author's Web site at
http://nancyvader.wordpress.com/

Contents

Foreword

In the last few years, the Completion Agenda has emerged as the overarching goal of the community college and will remain so at least for the coming decade. Never in the history of the community college movement has an idea so galvanized stakeholders—from the White House to the State House. Never have such large amounts of funding from philanthropic groups, such as the Bill and Melinda Gates Foundation and the Lumina Foundation for Education, been more generously funneled into a cause. Even as states struggle to survive in the face of sharply declining financial resources, the notion that community colleges can play a significant role in doubling the number of college completers is increasingly championed by the nation's community college leaders. The Completion Agenda is our 15 minutes of fame promised by Andy Warhol.

Community colleges are the right institutions to take on the task of completion; they have the right philosophy, the right programs, the right students, and they are strategically located in the right places. The challenge is clear: create learning environments and student success pathways that can, in the next two decades, double the number of students who complete, with marketplace value, a certificate or an associate's degree, or who transfer to earn a bachelor's degree. And ensure that these pathways work for the large number of students who are underprepared, from lower socio-economic backgrounds, and first-generation college students (O'Banion, 2011).

"Student success matters. College completion matters. And teaching and learning—the heart of student success—matter." (Center for Community College Student Engagement, 2010)

Teaching and learning designed to increase student success and college completion work best when supported by two foundational concepts: student engagement and active collaborative classroom experience:

> Research shows that more actively engaged students are, the more likely they are to learn, to persist in college, and to attain their academic goals. Student engagement, therefore, is an important metric for assessing the quality of colleges' educational practices and identifying ways colleges can help more students succeed. (Center for Community College Student Engagement, 2010)

> If we are to substantially increase college completion, especially among low-income students, we must focus on improving success in the classroom, particularly during a student's first year. We must be sensitive to the supports low-income students need to be successful in college, and lead efforts to dramatically improve their classroom experience. (Tinto, 2011)

Students can enjoy elegant and modern educational facilities. They can access the very latest in technological innovation. They can navigate educational pathways crafted from the most promising and high impact practices. Financial support can free them from the limitations of poverty. National and state policies can create conditions that provide opportunities available only to the most fortunate. But, if we cannot guarantee that students will engage with the most effective teaching and learning experiences in the classroom, we will fail to meet the goals of the Completion Agenda, and, indeed all of the laudable goals we have set for our students and our colleges.

A new book by my friend and colleague, Nancy Vader-McCormick, is the best guarantee I have seen in a long time that "students will engage with the most effective teaching and learning experiences in the classroom" if the nation's community college teachers will embrace the ideas and lessons from *The Engaged Teacher: What Works with Today's Students*. Nancy is very creative in the way she weaves together several distinct voices that give this book power and energy. She taps the latest resources from research and the existing literature on exemplary teaching and exemplary teachers. But she makes this information come alive by a continuing narrative of her own personal and formidable teaching experience over several decades. Furthermore, she enhances the summaries of research and citations from authorities with perspectives of 100 outstanding teachers and 200 representative students. She caps it off by sprinkling in every chapter a series of provocative questions and exercises to engage the reader in self reflection and action.

In addition to the very practical and useful information she shares in every chapter, Nancy has created a model framework for further research and consideration by scholars and practitioners. In The Engaged Teaching and Learning Model, she suggests a definition of engaged teaching and learning: "The process in which both teachers and students interact and actively participate in learning that helps them reach their desired goals." A simply stated but profound definition that undergirds this entire book.

Nancy Vader-McCormick is an authentic voice, seasoned and tempered in the fires of the teaching and learning experience; she has been on the firing line, on the ground, and in the trenches. In this book, she has transcended her experience as a practitioner to become a scholar, an author, a mentor — but always a teacher who wants to make passionate connections with her students and her readers.

Terry O'Banion, PhD

President Emeritus, League for Innovation in the Community College and Senior Advisor, Programs in Higher Education Walden University

Introduction

Whether you are new to teaching, or a seasoned faculty member with many years on the job, or somewhere in between, this book will help you discover fresh ideas for good teaching and revisit good teaching practices.

Good teaching has become more important now than ever before due to increased demands for improving educational outcomes plus the need to engage the modern, diverse population of college students in deep and sustained learning that will help them succeed.

Teachers who employ some of the study findings and practical approaches presented in this book will:

- Understand the relationship between the students, the subject matter, themselves, and teaching practices that positively influence and sustain student learning.
- Reflectively examine and expand their teaching approaches to increase student engagement in deeper learning and increased responsibility.
- Learn effective ways of teaching to enhance overall student success by employing a wide variety of practical examples, strategies, and pedagogies.

The Engaged Teacher: What Works with Today's Students describes today's diverse and challenging college students, trends in the growth of postsecondary education, and the increased demand for accountability in education. It highlights evidence-based practices that drive research on how students learn. Additionally, this study includes a largely unexamined source: the experiences of today's typical college students. From this fresh perspective and unique synthesis, a new model of engaged teaching and learning emerges, based on research and practical strategies from the practices of 100 exemplary teachers and the perceptions of 200 typical students.

Given initiatives such as Achieving the Dream and the Completion Agenda, community colleges and effective teaching have become national priorities for the next decade. Community colleges, experiencing a surge in growth, now enroll nearly half of all undergraduates in the U.S.

Much of the research, feedback, and strategies in *The Engaged Teacher* draws heavily from the scholar-practitioners teaching diverse students at community colleges. This study is one of the first to respond to cries from foundations such as Lumina and Gates, and from the current administration, to increase the number of community college graduates in the U.S. *The Engaged Teacher* presents tested strategies for engaging students in deep and sustained learning that are key to the Student Success Agenda.

I write this book as a practitioner because I admire and have empathy for both today's faculty and students. As a professor of communication, with over 25 years of college teaching and corporate training experience, now teaching at a large, diverse Midwest community college, I continually seek ways to become a better teacher. Early in my teaching career, I struggled with the questions all new teachers grapple with, such as: How will I keep the students engaged for the entire class period? How will I know they are learning? How do I handle classroom management issues? Have I thoroughly studied, prepared, and chosen the material, the substance of the class?

I still wrestle with some of these questions every semester, because things change. Students change. I've changed. Information and technology have exploded and changed *what* and *how* we teach. Much of what we do as teachers has changed. But, for me, and for many other teachers I surveyed for this book, the most important question semester after semester, student after student, still boils down to how do I help students learn?

The purpose of this book is to highlight the principles, beliefs, and strategies that have emerged from the studies *and* practices of exemplary teachers. Every single day, today's teachers face new challenges and questions about what helps students learn. And, teachers often work without much discussion or feedback from their teaching colleagues, whether they teach in a classroom or online.

While discussions of good teaching often occur between professional educators alone, the perceptions of students are overlooked. This book combines the voices of teachers and students with discoveries of leading scholars to define what it takes to teach well. I've examined what exemplary, hard-working teachers do that helps explain their effectiveness, in order to shed light on what engages students in learning.

What makes this book different from others is that three fourths of the teachers in this study are from community colleges. I chose community colleges because they place primary focus on teaching. Of the community college teachers included in this study, nearly half teach at districts that are institutional members of the League for Innovation in the Community College. The League, an organization committed to improving community colleges, is internationally recognized as a dynamic and influential catalyst in the higher education.

The teachers selected to participate have been recognized by their colleagues or students for their effective teaching. Ninety percent received institutional or national teaching awards. One hundred fifty award-winning teachers were sent surveys; 100 responded (67% return rate). In addition, 10 of the responding teachers were interviewed in depth, and 15 were observed in the classroom.

Using content analysis, the themes emerging from this research were used to shape The Engaged Teaching and Learning Model. The model is supplemented with snapshots of stories presented by a few teachers and students in real college classrooms, stories that can't be found in most books on teaching.

The second feature that makes this book different from previous studies and books on effective teaching is the inclusion of college students' voices and perspectives. The students, 80% of whom had attended a community college at some point, were surveyed at varying ages and stages of their academic experiences, including some who were out of college for a few years. Of 240 student surveys, 202 were returned (84% return rate). In addition, I conducted an online focus group with 15 students.

The student data, detailed in Chapter Four, was analyzed both quantitatively and qualitatively to draw out themes relating to both the literature and the themes that emerged from the teacher surveys. The student perspectives, emerging from within the context of the compelling demographics of today's students, represent a diverse mix: community college, four-year university, transfer, reverse transfer, returning adult, Millennial, and "Generation Me" students.

The research approach for this book sought a combination of evidence, much like Bain's (2004) examination of teachers in *What the*

Best College Teachers Do and *Practical Magic: On the Front Lines of Teaching Excellence*, by Roueche, Milliron, and Roueche (2003). There is no attempt to capture all of the significant and current studies on teaching and learning; rather, an overview of important studies is presented.

Although this book is aimed at helping faculty, it is also for those supporting or supervising teachers: faculty developers, department chairs, and other academic administrators promoting teaching and improving learning. However, it is not a beginning primer for constructing syllabi or a listing of desired traits of great teachers. Rather, it describes a variety of time-tested principles and practices used by exemplary teachers who engage students in learning.

The Engaged Teacher demonstrates that effective teaching is not a result of mere talent, but relies heavily on skills that can be learned and strategies that can be employed to enhance the classroom experience.

My own journey as a teacher and student is a component of this book. My personal narratives, included in many chapters, are an undeniable part of my own story as a teacher. Given the self-reflective nature of the teaching profession, it is crucial to place my lived experiences within the context of this study of teaching effectiveness. The personal narratives, interspersed throughout this book, are kept as clearly distinct as possible from the analysis of the teacher and student perceptions. My intent is that the autobiographical narratives will help illustrate the challenges raised throughout this book.

This book includes three major parts. Part One, "Contemporary Teaching Challenges," is composed of Chapters One through Four, which provide the context and rationale for why we need to improve the quality of teaching in higher education, including feedback from students. Part Two, "Engaged Teachers Meet Today's Challenges," consisting of Chapters Five through Seven, presents the feedback, perspectives and practices emerging from the exemplary teachers participating in this study. Part Three, Sustaining Engaged Teaching and Learning, including Chapters Eight, Nine, and the Epilogue, presents 75 ideas and strategies for engaged teaching and learning and some final thoughts on engaged teaching.

Here is a breakdown of the chapters:

Chapter 1: The changing higher education environment with challenges posed by today's diverse students is examined.

Chapter 2: The rationale for why teaching matters is presented, with a focus on community college faculty and students.

Chapter 3: An overview of the research on effective teaching and student learning is presented and integrated with The Engaged Teaching and Learning Model.

Chapter 4: The feedback from students is presented, along with relevant studies on what students say about teachers who help them learn.

Chapter 5: The insights from engaged teachers demonstrating how they understand and help students create learning connections are explained.

Chapter 6: Presents practices that engage students in the subject through active learning. These are based on the practices of exemplary teachers in the study.

Chapter 7: The insights and reflective practices of the exemplary teachers illustrated through classroom, and self-appraisal strategies.

Chapter 8: Presents 50 of the best ideas and strategies for engaged teaching and learning captured in this study.

Chapter 9: Presents 25 ideas for engaged teaching and learning with a focus on collegiality and community.

Epilogue: Concludes the study's analysis of "best" teaching practice findings.

I have made every attempt to attribute accurately, but some teaching strategies are spread informally or are part of common good practices so that specific sources may not exist or be known. If I have misrepresented someone's practice or ideas, please contact me so I can correct it in a future edition and/or post a correction on my website at http://nancyvader.wordpress.com/teaching/

I hope this book opens your mind and heart to the lasting life-changing lessons from engaged teachers presented in it.

Acknowledgements

I would not be a teacher without the many inspiring teachers I've been lucky enough to have as mentors and friends. And, I certainly would not have written a book without the support, stories, and inspiration from hundreds of teachers I have met, studied with, laughed with, and learned from over the five-year span it took to complete this book. I am deeply indebted to them and to the students who shared their stories, observations, and insights with me.

Also, I am especially thankful to the following colleagues and friends who encouraged, supported, and assisted me in the production of this book:

- Terry O'Banion, who wrote the foreword and first introduced me to the concept of the learning college with its focus on student learning; his writings and speeches have been sources of rich information and inspiration.
- Nancy Manning and Ralph Forsberg, who patiently read and competently edited and formatted numerous versions of the manuscript; in addition, they both challenged my thinking and raised critical questions that prompted me to reconstruct and improve several key sections of the manuscript.
- Elaine Stephens and Maryann Rosenthal, who gave me extensive guidance and tips about writing this book as well as lifelong encouragement, friendship, love and support; their writings and honest reactions to my work challenged me to think more deeply about the needs of students and teachers.
- Marcia Potter, who read early versions of the manuscript and compelled me to broaden my thinking in terms of the audience for this book; her belief in my ability to write combined with helpful suggestions made the work immensely better.

- Murlene McKinnon, who presented me with my first opportunity to teach in the real world, years of mentoring in teaching and training, and an unwavering belief in my ability to make a difference as a teacher.
- Late friend and educator, Julia Berg, who encouraged me through every stage of my life and the writing of this book; her advice to "write the book!" kept me going.
- Doug Dollar of New Forums Press, who provided interest and belief in the book, as well as expert guidance and timely encouragement, both of which helped to bring this project to life.

Whether they knew it or not, numerous colleagues, mentors, and friends have provided meaningful examples and hours of rich conversation about teaching and learning that guided the direction of this manuscript. Their inspiration and support continues to influence my beliefs and teaching. Special thanks to these teachers and colleagues: Skip Renker, Julia Fogarty, Barb Handley-Miller, Linda Plackowski, Karen Wilson, Gail Hoffman-Johnson, Elaine Karls, Peggy Barber, Bobbi Allen, Renee Hoppe, Sharon Bernthal, Tracy Spring, Darien Ripple, Nancy Laughner, Jeremy Kilar, Ray Roberts, Pat Eggleston, and Val Harrold.

In addition, I have had the honor to work under the leadership of three outstanding presidents at Delta College from whom I have learned much that shaped my journey in higher education: Donald Carlyon, Peter Boyse, and Jean Goodnow.

Finally, I owe a special debt of gratitude and love to my parents, grandparents, and family — my first teachers — for providing me with the foundation for learning and hard work, sustained by their unconditional love and support. My dear sister Carol buoyed me with her company at the family farmhouse where I did most of the writing for this book. My husband John McCormick's example of steady discipline to create in his studio inspired me to create on my laptop. Our youngest daughter Megan, a college student herself during the time I wrote this book, typed dozens of surveys and compiled data summaries for me. Their love, support, and belief in me helped make this book a reality.

Part One

Contemporary Teaching Challenges

Chapter One

The Changing Landscape

Education is not filling a bucket, but lighting a fire.
— William Butler Yeats

Teaching and learning will become even more visible and more significant as instructors respond to the overwhelming challenge of providing successful educational opportunities for the most diverse group of college students in the history of the world.
— Terry O'Banion

Author Narrative: Today's Students

Chantelle, a second-year student at a mid-size community college, is struggling to keep up her grades and stay focused on her college goals. She is taking a full load, commuting to college three days a week, and working part-time at a department store. As a single mom with two young children, she doesn't have time for study groups or tutoring, and has never been to see an instructor during office hours. Frustrated and stressed, she says, "I try to stay organized and focus on my school work, but sometimes I just get overloaded and do poorly on a test or assignment. And, I really don't feel connected to the school or the other students. It's hard to keep motivated."

Brian, previously a freshman at a large state university, was majoring in photography. He was a top academic student in high school and had relished going away to a big university just like his older brother and sister. A few weeks into his first semester, however, he stopped going to most of his classes. He bombed academically, dropped out, and moved home after his first semester. His parents insisted he stay in college so he enrolled in the local community college as a reverse transfer student. He also enrolled in substance abuse rehabilitation counseling and kicked an addiction he'd picked up at the university.

Tina, after two years at a community college, transferred as a junior to a well-known private university as a business major. She enjoyed the small class size and personal contact with her community college instructors, and is having a hard time adjusting to a bigger, less personal school. "The faculty here at the university teach differently than my community college teachers," she explains. "I feel like I'm not relating to the professors and where they're coming from in most of my classes. And, it's so hard to meet people as an outsider."

Millions of today's students such as Chantelle, Brian, and Tina, described above, are among the biggest challenges today's teachers face. They are the most diverse and academically challenging array of students ever encountered by faculty in higher education settings. Today's students want and need teachers who engage them in learning. They are the reason for this book.

Reflect and respond. As you continue reading Chapter 1, consider the questions listed below and reflect on your own experiences as a teacher:

- How have the students you are teaching changed over the years?
- What, if anything, do you do differently as a teacher than you've done in the past?
- Where is most of your energy as a teacher going right now?

Why We Need Engaged Teachers

Globalization and open door access have filled our classrooms with learners reflecting such a dizzying array of backgrounds and academic preparedness that teachers are often hard pressed to find a collective starting point or the commonalities that create a sense of community. Abundant information at split-second access redefined what students should be learning and created unprecedented opportunities for academic dishonesty.

—Elizabeth Barkley

When a school year ends, I look forward to lots of reading, previewing new media, attending a workshop or two, traveling, and re-energizing myself during the break. That's one of the benefits of teaching: you get periodic breaks from the classroom to step back and regroup. I've never talked to a teacher who didn't need it. But, very little of that is happening in my teaching life right now.

Instead, I am sitting in a computer lab on a sunny summer afternoon trying to learn the new course management system my college has adopted. I desperately need to master it and complete over 20 hours of training during the semester break. The new course management system is mandatory for all of the courses taught online and highly suggested for the regular face-to-face courses, too. I have six different course preps, two of which I teach online, so I'm feeling a real sense of urgency here, not to mention a sense of frustration. I'm retaking some of the training modules because I don't think they "stuck" the first time I took them.

For me, sitting in a computer training lab and learning new applications and programs without my own personal laptop is like trying to cook a gourmet meal in a toaster oven. Toaster oven or not, all I know is I've got to complete this training and get all of my six course sites up and running over the summer break. What a change from the work I used to do over the semester break!

Change? Yes, that's what characterizes the landscape of education now: change driven by new information, technology, and students. Expectations and demands on faculty and their development have changed as well. One of the biggest changes in professional development for teachers has been the erosion of meaningful time spent talking about teaching among colleagues and across departments. Instead, this precious time is now spent primarily talking about policies, procedures, organizational changes, or in training sessions to stay up to date on the newest technology.

Just this past school year, a colleague and I offered to facilitate a discussion about teaching during one of our monthly departmental faculty meetings. This topic was a big change from the usual agenda and type of meeting we endured each month. My colleague led the first teaching discussion, which was a big hit, and the faculty asked for more. So, we asked for another time block on the agenda the next month to continue the teaching discussion. Unfortunately, we were denied the 20-minute time block because "there are too many other important issues we need to address."

As is the case too often now in higher education circles, our need for significant dialogue about teaching and learning was placed at the bottom of the list of faculty and institutional issues. Yet, clearly, faculty discussions about teaching, learning, and re-lated professional development need to be more of a priority.

Faculty development is more crucial than ever as we embrace changes and upgrade our skills to serve today's increasingly diverse and underprepared student body. Like our students, we need to stay engaged in our own learning. We need to stay engaged as teachers in order to reach today's students. It's not good enough to merely be subject matter experts. To be a good teacher today, we need to be experts on teaching and learning, on our students, in our subject matter, and to stay up to date on the newest technology.

Now, more than ever, we need engaged teachers to keep pace with these changes *and* help today's students learn. What is needed, and what this book provides, is a reinvigorated focus on the role of faculty in engaging students in learning that *sticks*.

Changes and Challenges in Today's Colleges

If there is one thing we can count on in education today, it is change: changes in attitudes about degrees, changes in traditional routes to college, changes in students, changes in technology — and changes in the needs and demands of today's students. These changes are reshaping today's educational landscape.

Changing attitudes about college degrees. A college degree is more important now than ever. Despite the recent study by the Pew Research Center (2011) that found more than half of Americans do not think a college education is worth the money, the fact is that those with bachelor degrees earn a great deal more on average than college dropouts over the course of a 40-year working life. College graduates earn an estimated $550,000 more throughout their lifetimes than high school graduates, even when figuring in the foregone earnings and cost of attending college (Pew Research Center, 2011).

Changing traditional routes to a college degree. While demand is increasing for all types of post-secondary education, the traditional route to a college degree is changing, as noted in a National Center for Education Statistics (NCES) report (2007). Currently, nearly one third of all college and university students who drop out after their first year and one half never graduate at all. Completion rates are worse for minority students and students enrolled in remedial classes. Half of U.S. college graduates travel the so-called "nontraditional" route to a degree, attending two or more schools. Many "drop down" from four-year schools to attend less expensive schools like community colleges, where enrollment is booming.

Changes in students. Predominant in today's classrooms are the Millennial and Generation Me students. Twenge (2006) studied those born in the 1970s to 1990s; this 30-year span encompasses today's young people now ranging in age from middle school to 30-something adults. Twenge's (2006) findings on Generation Me, from the largest intergenerational research study ever conducted, characterizes these students as:

- Tolerant, confident, open-minded, ambitious, cynical, lonely, and anxious
- Appreciating directness
- Displaying a decline of manners, politeness, social rules
- Overloaded with information and technology as a way of life
- Possessing high self-esteem and low self-control
- Reporting they learn best by doing and will work harder with praise and recognition

Howe and Strauss (2000) studied what is known as the "Millennial generation," those born between 1982 and 2002. They found this cohort to be racially and ethnically diverse, team-oriented, pressured, achieving, and civic-minded. Both the Generation Me and Millennial groups pose unique challenges and opportunities to higher education.

Focusing on the motivation and expectations of today's students, scholar Weimer's (2002) description evokes an image of disengaged students recognizable to most faculty:

How would you characterize today's college students? Empowered, confident, self-motivated learners? That is not how I would describe mine. The ones in my classes are hopeful but generally anxious and tentative. They all want classes to be easy but expect that most will be hard. They wish their major (whatever it might be) did not require math, science, or English courses. A good number will not speak in class unless called on. Most like, want, indeed need teachers who tell them exactly what to do. Education is something done unto them. It frequently involves stress, anxiety, and other forms of discomfort. (p. 23)

Changes in technology. Another challenge for faculty, especially those at community colleges, comes from the increased use and availability of various technologies. More so than at most university settings, faculty members at community colleges are expected to be proficient in the use of a variety of new instructional technologies. Many of these technology changes include changing course management systems, updating presentation and web software, adapting lab and classroom technology, and developing and using new media, blogs, videos, and supplemental websites for classes.

New technologies are transforming how higher education delivers courses. The increase in distance education is growing at community colleges where flexible and affordable online courses are especially appealing to displaced workers and job hunters. It is estimated that the increase in online enrollments have not yet peaked at community colleges, given their open door policy intended to accommodate diverse students and new programs aimed at stimulating the economy. This growth raises additional challenges and questions about teaching and learning, including:

- Appropriateness of courses redesigned from face-to-face to online formats
- Quality control of online courses
- Qualifications and technology competencies for online faculty
- Assessment of courses delivered online

These changes and challenges prompt faculty to seek out ways to improve student learning and become the best teachers they can possibly be. These changes and challenges can be met by faculty willing to do what they ask students to do: engage in learning. Just as students need to be aware of how they are learning, teachers need to be aware of how they are teaching and the effect it has on student learning.

Modern teaching challenges. The fact is, many students today are academically and emotionally unprepared, and therefore at risk in the classroom. Their unpreparedness influences their confidence level, ability, and attitude as learners. Teachers need to muster as much passion as possible to meet the challenge of engaging at-risk students.

Weimer (2002) explains:

> Students now arrive at college less well prepared than they once did. They often lack solid basic skills and now work many hours to pay for college and sometimes a car. . . . Many students lack confidence in themselves as learners and do not make responsible learning decisions . . . . Having little self-confidence and busy lives motivates students to look for easy educational options, not ones that push them hard . . . . Obviously, these descriptions are not characteristic of all students, but most faculty quickly agree that teaching college students today is far more challenging than it once was. (pp. 95-96)

For many college and university teachers today, teaching is particularly challenging due to the new "average" college student as described by Mellow and Heelan (2008):

> The average American student no longer corresponds to a traditional stereotype of "college student." It would be as accurate to think of a middle-aged African-American woman who squeezes college into two evenings a week while she maintains a full-time job and cares for her family as it is to imagine a 20-year-old white man drinking beer with his fraternity brothers before the football game. (p. 8)

Most of us, particularly those of us who teach a large proportion of first-generation college students at community colleges, know that we must understand what such students need from us to help them succeed as learners. Students need passionate teachers who create the conditions for engaging them from the moment they walk into the classroom until they walk across the stage to receive their diplomas at graduation.

Summary

Teachers are teaching the most diverse student body in history while being challenged with larger class sizes, fewer resources, and changing technologies. Today's faculty must meet the challenge of teaching effectively and engaging students in learning. Teachers need to create environments and conditions in which students learn and thrive. This is crucial, as the mix of diversity and academic preparation today's students bring to college classrooms, exemplified in the six-million-plus students attending community colleges, makes college teaching more challenging than ever — and dictates the need for engaged teaching.

Author Narrative: What Brought Me to Teaching

My personal journey to teaching was not at all a linear path. Rather, it was a road full of curves, bumps, and detours, all of which eventually led me to teaching. I had not considered teaching as a career while I was in college. As a liberal arts student majoring in communication, I wasn't sure what kind of career path I would follow after graduation.

Ironically, I did end up working at a community college as an admissions counselor right after graduating from college. After a few years, I became the coordinator of 30 off-campus centers in the community where the college held classes and provided support services.

During that time, I earned my MA degree and was encouraged to pursue my PhD, which I did. Despite my administrative career path, I was drawn to teaching but scared and filled with inadequacies. I'd taken several classes from some of the finest faculty at my college, and was fascinated with their mastery in the classroom. Was it talent, technique, personality, experience? I didn't know, but I knew I wanted to do what they were doing. I just didn't know how.

So, I started "subbing" for various faculty members at my campus and discovered I loved teaching. I felt as though I had unleashed a passion in my life. I felt like a horse at the gate of the Kentucky Derby, ready to run and eager to be part of the pack, but running as a wild card.

At last, I was asked to substitute for a faculty member I greatly admired. She was like the rock star of teaching at the college. Despite her petite size, she strode into the classroom with the confidence and command of a 10-foot giant. On her way to the front of the room, she always commented to students with remarks that included "Good morning" or "How are you?" or "Nice backpack, I like that color." Quickly, yet effectively and thoroughly making eye contact with what seemed like every student in the classroom, she'd grin and say, "Welcome, I'm so glad to see you all." You could tell she meant it. You just knew she was going to be a great teacher. And, she was.

Years later, as a teacher myself, I realized that the most important things I learned from observing her were to apply almost everything said or done in class to some critical aspects of students' lives, to regularly connect with students in ways that positively acknowledged them, and to provide abundant feedback to students about their learning.

The classes I taught for her went well, and she received positive feedback, kidding me, "Don't be so good that they'll want me to stay away and want you to take over!"

That joke came to pass, in a way, because the following semester she became ill and required surgery, and asked me to take over two of her classes. I wanted to do it although I had a full-time administrative position at the college, plus taught classes as an adjunct in another department. And, I was very pregnant—seven months to be exact. But, it worked out that I could teach her classes up until a couple weeks before my due date, which was when she could return to campus to teach.

The classes went well and subbing was a great opportunity for me to gain more teaching experience. The only problem was that I went into labor on what was supposed to be the day of my last class. When my husband and I got to the hospital and saw the doctor, I said, "The baby's not due for two weeks . . . this was supposed to be my last day of work!"

The doctor chuckled and said, "Don't worry, it will be a day of work. Labor, that is." Of course, it was!

That semester of teaching for my mentor created a desire for the classroom. I continued to teach as an adjunct faculty member at a nearby university as well as at the community college.

A year later, some unique circumstances propelled me into teaching full-time. My mentor decided suddenly to retire from her teaching position at the college, and she recommended that I replace her, saying, "Nancy's a good teacher and she cares about students the same way I do."

I was ecstatic when the college offered me the full-time teaching position for the year. They stressed that the full-time teaching experience would be an asset if I were to apply for the tenure track position in the near future. "What did I have to lose?" I thought. So, despite the words of a colleague ringing in the back of my mind, "Be careful about the way they offer it to you," I accepted with enthusiasm.

It was a steep learning curve as I taught a full-time load with four different preps, but I dug in and managed to stay at least a week ahead of the students. I kept asking myself, "What would my mentor do?" My colleagues were helpful and encouraging. I loved teaching. I loved the students. And, I loved the challenges. I was learning so much; the feedback from students and colleagues was positive, and I enjoyed classroom teaching.

The dream ended abruptly near the end of the school year. The tenure track position for the job I was doing was posted and I applied. Weeks passed and I wasn't hearing much about the hiring process.

I started to inquire and received mixed messages: "The position description was still being tweaked . . . The committee hasn't been able to meet . . . . Affirmative action issues are being discussed." And so on. I was getting the message that I may not be a qualified candidate for the position I'd been filling for the year. And, at the same time, I discovered I was pregnant. I decided not to mention my pregnancy at work until I knew more about the selection process. So, I kept on teaching and trusting the institution, people, and processes that had been my place of employment for 12 years. Then, I received bad news. Twice.

I went into my obstetrician's office for my second appointment and ultrasound, just over three months into my pregnancy. After several attempts to find a heartbeat, my doctor murmured,

"We have to send you over to the hospital for additional tests . . . this might not be a viable pregnancy . . . I can't locate a heart-beat."

No! I could not believe it. I lost my baby. And, six weeks later, I lost my job. I received notification from the college that the faculty job description I'd been performing for the past year had been changed and my qualifications no longer fit the redescribed position. For the first time in my adult life, I was without a full-time job and I had lost two things I loved at the same time—my baby and my teaching position. It was time to regroup.

Reflect and respond. Reflect upon your own path to becoming a teacher as you respond to the following questions:
- Why did you become a teacher?
- Who was your mentor and how did they influence you?
- How have changes in students prompted changes in your teaching practice?
- What aspects of teaching are most challenging to you?

Engaged Teaching Strategy Ia: What Motivates Students to Learn?

Directions: Early in the semester, break students into small groups of four to six and ask them to brainstorm a list of responses to these two questions:
- What are things that keep you motivated and focused in school?
- What things can students and teacher do in this class to encourage motivation?

Post large sheets of newsprint on the classroom walls and ask students to write their responses on the sheets. After a few minutes of posting, ask each group to report out. Discuss similarities, themes, and ways students and teacher can contribute to a motivating classroom environment.

Extended Engaged Teaching Strategy Ib: Motivation/Concept Showcase

Directions: Ask students to bring in a personal artifact or a YouTube video (link) illustrating motivation (or a concept related to course content) to the next class period. First, have students share their examples in small groups and report out by showing some of the examples the group found most interesting. Follow up with a discussion of motivation and how it influences learning, or the concept and why it is important.

Chapter Two

Teaching Matters

Teachers possess the power to create conditions that can help students learn a great deal — or keep them from learning much at all.

— Parker Palmer

Author Narrative: I Never Intended to be a Teacher

I never intended to be a teacher. Growing up on a farm in rural Michigan in the 1960s, despite the fact that I had to help out in the fields with my older brother, I had lots of time in the summer to read and daydream and wander through the woods considering the course my life would take when I left the farm. As a young girl, my dream was to leave the farm and travel the world as a missionary doctor. During my childhood I read the entire series of the Nancy Drew young amateur detective books, figuring it was more than coincidence that our names were both Nancy, and fantasized endlessly about becoming a Nancy Drew clone in my own life. Our lives couldn't have been more different, but reading took me away from the farm as I escaped to the glamorous life of mystery, travel, and adventure in each book I read.

One of the other major influences on my childhood was how much time I spent in church. My grandmother, who was the church pianist, never missed a service, and I was her regular tagalong. Because I loved spending time at her house, I ended up going with her to church a lot by default, although I think maybe she had something to do with me being there on church days.

Grandma also was a Sunday School teacher and very involved with an organization called the World Gospel Mission. In her piano room, she had a big, framed world map that she pushed little plastic colored pins in to illustrate where all the missionaries she knew were stationed. I thought it was amazing that she knew these people who were teaching and saving other people all over the world. She'd share stories and books with me about what they were doing in those faraway places. Most of them were doctors or nurses or preachers or teachers. When she talked about them, I could hear a kind of longing in her voice, sort of the way I felt when I read the Nancy Drew books and dreamed I was Nancy Drew. She would show me the envelopes addressed to the missionaries in distant places where she sent them money. When she mailed them, she put a green pushpin on the map next to their location. While Grandma was sending money to missionaries, I was spending what little money I had on Nancy Drew books and saving the rest for when I was old enough to go away, leave the farm, and live a life of adventure somewhere else!

As I entered high school, I wasn't sure at all what I wanted to be when I grew up. I remember my favorite teacher asking me, "What will you study after you graduate and go on to college?"

I replied, "Our family doesn't go to college."

Years later, my teacher told me how stunned she was by my response. Somehow, however, she knew how to plant the seed at the right time and how to help open up my limited thinking to the possibility of college.

No one in my family had ever gone to college. I wasn't sure how to go about selecting a college and I was even more confused about what to major in if I went to college. So, I pored over books and catalogues in the cubbyhole sized guidance office (converted from a broom closet) on a regular basis, but any kind of certainty eluded me.

I scheduled an appointment with the part-time guidance counselor/coach/government teacher at the school. I hoped he could shed some light on this unknown territory for me and provide tools to help me navigate how to choose a college and career. Instead, he gave me disinterested advice, after he fielded several coaching-related phone calls during the first 15 minutes of our appointment time. Finally, when the phone calls subsided, he turned to me.

The school counselor leaned back in his chair and crossed his huge arms above his enormous belly. He scrunched up his wrinkled shirt sleeves to reveal mounds of coarse dark hair that matched his thick bushy eyebrows. His slightly tinted aviator glasses, smeared with what looked like chalk dust, hung low on his nose and bounced up and down when he said, "Well, how are you doing in science and math?"

"Okay," I responded, "but I really love my English class..."

"Have you looked at Hurley School of Nursing? It's close by, just about an hour away. They have a two-year RN program..."

"Well, I really don't think I want to be a nurse..."

I don't think he was listening to any of my protests as he reached up on the shelf and pulled out a brochure for the nearby nursing school. Handing it to me, he said, "Nursing will give you something to fall back on."

"What was I going to be falling from?" I wondered.

"BRRRRRRRRRRRRRRRING!" The ebony phone rattled once. He scooped it up as he waved me out of his office. As I left, I knew I'd never go back to see him again. Somehow, I'd figure it all out. I tossed the brochure for nursing school in the trash.

After high school, I did go away to college. The first day was not at all like I expected. The year was 1973, and I was a freshman at a large university in Michigan. Bell-bottomed blue jeans, sandals, and long straight hair parted down the middle. The important thing was to look cool and act cool. Fit in. Be accepted. Make friends. Adjust. Although I didn't have a clue. I came from a lineage of Midwestern farmers and fishermen. As a first-generation college student, I was both terrified and thrilled to be in college.

Reflect and respond. I hope that the memories I've shared have helped to transport you back to your own early years as a student. Gently pull yourself into the experiences you had in school. Picture yourself as the student you were at the time. Take a few moments to jot down, or discuss, your reflections as you consider these questions:

- What were your dreams as a child?
- What did you want to be when you "grew up?"
- What things do you remember most about school? What is most vivid?
- Who influenced or inspired you?
- What originally brought you to teach the subject you are teaching right now?
- What obstacles or barriers did you encounter along the way?

Teachers Make a Difference

A good teacher is one who helps students make a passionate connection to learning.
— Terry O'Banion

Simply but powerfully stated: *teachers matter.* Studies confirm that teacher quality more heavily influences student performance than does race, class, or school of the student (Nye, Konstantopoulos & Hedges, 2004). According to a report by the American Council on Education (1999), "the success of the student depends most of all on the quality of the teacher. We know from empirical data what our intuition has always told us: Teachers make a difference. We now know that teachers make *the* difference" (p. 5).

Yet, when talking to today's college students, they disclose that they often register for courses based on reasons other than teacher quality. Students admit spending time surfing ratemyprofessor.com website for instructor information. This site—comprised of students' anonymous ratings of instructors, including a "hot pepper" rating for perceived "hotness"—has become a guide for thousands of students as they register for courses. Although many teachers prefer to think that students seek them out and register for their class because they heard what a good teacher they are, student comments like these jolt them into reality:

- "This time slot for Math fits perfectly into my schedule. I'm not a morning person, so I really lucked out finding this class offered from 2-5 p.m."

- "I heard that you really don't have to read the book in this class; it's all in the Power Point slides."
- "I can't believe *she's* a 'Hot Pepper'..."

Despite the paths students take to arrive, they land in our classrooms and we strive to engage them in significant learning experiences. They need engaged teachers who challenge and connect with them in ways that result in significant learning and create responsible learners.

Studies (Bain, 2004; Brookfield, 2006) generally show that students engage in learning with teachers who know their subjects, know their students, and know how to teach. Students respond favorably to teachers who are knowledgeable, credible, and committed professionals. Students relate to and respect teachers who are deeply connected to their students, their subjects, and themselves. And, many studies (Barkley, 2010; Weimer, 2002) are now demonstrating that students learn best from teachers who create meaningful active learning environments that engage students applying the subject and helping them understand how they are learning.

Here is what a community college freshman has to say about teachers in The Engaged Teacher Study:

> If a teacher walks into the classroom and just talks, and we don't talk, I put myself in a shell and sit back. Some students don't have enough confidence to raise their hands. It's the teacher's job to get students interacting with each other so they aren't afraid to ask questions. In my best classes, we had discussions and listened to everybody. The teacher cared about what we learned, how we learned, whether we understood or not, and how we felt about a situation. In those classes, I learned that I had a voice.

Reflect and respond. As you examine the realities about today's students, think about the teachers who engaged you when you were a student. Think about yourself as a student, especially when you were in college. As you do so, reflect on the following question:
- Who were the truly good teachers in your life?

Take a few minutes to think about these teachers. List them, picture them, and re-visit what they did and what they said. Try to remember how they made you feel. Ask yourself what kind of influence they may have had in your life. Think about how they looked and how they conducted class. Connect with your memory of the truly good teachers you've had in your life and then

- List those truly good teachers by name.

How many teachers did you remember and list? If you're like most people, you probably listed somewhere between one and five. Most of us can count the truly good teachers we've had on just one hand. That's amazing when you consider that even if you only counted the number of teachers in your K to 12 education, you'd have around 75. *Seventy-five teachers.* After your bachelor's degree, you'd have well over 100 teachers; a master's degree would push the number close to 150. Yet, most of us can only name a very few teachers we've had whom we consider truly good teachers.

The truly good teachers most of us remember are the ones who challenged and engaged us in learning that helped us connect with the subject in ways that resulted in significant learning. It is likely that those teachers believed in us and in our ability to learn. No doubt they knew their subjects inside and out. And, they probably involved us in an active learning environment where we felt we were supported and challenged.

Truly engaged teachers ignite students' learning, encourage their growth and foster responsibility through a variety of approaches. Truly engaged teachers keep students actively involved and thinking about what and how they learn.

Here is how a college student in The Engaged Teacher Study describes truly good teachers:

> A good teacher motivates, captivates and makes learning interesting. They reach every person's learning level and relate the subject to the real world. They make you want to come to class. They know their subject, and are very passionate and enthusiastic about the material and about teaching. They do more than teach the class material, they teach you about life.

Now, return to your list of good teachers. Picture them in your mind. Transport yourself back to their classroom. Remember what it was like for you to have them as your teacher. Reflect on your own experiences with teachers in your life. Then, ask yourself the following questions:
- What did they do to help me learn?
- What kind of impact or influence have they had on my life?
- What kind of student was I with these teachers?
- What kinds of things did they do in the classroom?
- How did those teachers make me feel?
- What were my strengths?
- What did I see the teachers do that I've never seen another teacher do?

Revisit your list of good teachers. If you have attended or teach at a community college, shift your focus specifically to those experiences as we examine the types of students that attend community colleges and the teachers that teach them.

Why Community College Teachers Matter

So many misunderstandings about our mission, our job, abound. Some think that we are simply an extension of high school; others that we are merely vocational schools. We need to render our work in a visible and authentic way to those who do not know first-hand what it is we do. We need to construct for them, and perhaps for ourselves as well, an image of our work as intellectually rigorous and, yes, eminently practical. We need to tell our own stories and not rely on others to tell them for us.

— Howard Tinberg, CASE U.S. Professor of the Year Acceptance Speech

Today's struggling economy is driving a record number of students to community colleges that focus strongly on teaching. Over six million students attend community colleges in the United States. Community colleges now enroll 43%, or nearly half, of all U.S. college students (NCES, 2007). Several reasons drive the need to examine teaching effectiveness, especially in community colleges.

Community colleges differ from traditional four-year colleges in many ways. Two key characteristics of community colleges — open admissions and traditionally low tuition — attract diverse populations as they fulfill transfer, career, and basic skills functions for millions of students each year. Mellow and Heelan (2008) describe the challenge and opportunity such diversity poses:

> The average community college student, nationally, is 29, but ages range from 16 to 90-plus. This diversity brings with it immensely different expectations and needs on the part of students, as well as a richness that creates powerful learning environments. (p. 261)

The diversity of students enrolled in community colleges represents a microcosm of today's students at all institutions of higher education. They enter college with an assortment of life experiences and varying degrees of academic preparation. Some community college students are still in high school, some are ready to transfer to a university, and some hold advanced degrees. They are three to four times more likely than their four-year counterparts to need remedial classes, to delay their entry to college after graduating from high school, to be single parents, to have children, to work more than 30 hours a week, and to be financially independent.

Community colleges enroll the majority of students with the lowest levels of performance in higher education (Kane & Rouse, 1999); not surprisingly, these are the students most sensitive to the quality of instruction they receive. Students now entering community colleges are much more likely to require some form of developmental or remedial education than the overall population of entering college students.

Unfortunately, those students with greater developmental learning needs are less likely to persist in courses and succeed in college (Kuh, Kinzie, Schuh, & Whitt, 2005). In fact, of the students who took at least one remedial reading course in college, 70% did not earn a certificate or degree within eight years of enrollment (Kuh et al, 2005, p. 1).

The highly situational, challenging, and demanding nature of teaching in the community college is described by O'Banion in *Teaching and Learning in the Community College* (1994):

New instructors facing a class of community college students for the first time often find traditional teaching methods ineffective. What works for a class of high school students of the same age or a class of university students of similar socio-economic backgrounds and SAT scores often does not work in a class of community college students with no common denominator except membership in the human race. Given this diversity, it is no wonder the community college is called the 'teaching college,' and community college teachers are among the most creative innovators in all of higher education. (pp. 13-14)

The scenario described by O'Banion paints a picture of the many aspects of student diversity today's teachers face in the classroom. In addition, many of today's students are not well prepared or motivated for college. Credible and engaging teachers can help those students relate to the subject being taught and increase the likelihood they persist and succeed in college.

The value of studying good teaching, with emphasis on the methods employed to reach diverse learners such as those attending community colleges, is that it provides an ideal opportunity to discover approaches that can be applied to all of higher education.

Focus on teaching. Unlike universities where research is stressed, or K to 12 systems where discipline, standardized test scores, and other administrative standards can be key factors, the major focus for faculty at community colleges is *teaching*. As pointed out by O'Banion (1997), "In contrast to other institutions of higher education, the community college has always taken great pride in its commitment to teaching as its highest value" (p. 27).

Teaching loads. Community college faculty have much greater teaching loads than university faculty, and teach more classes each semester than any other sector of higher education.

Class size. Class size is another variable. At many universities, a professor or teaching assistant may have a class of 200 students crammed in a lecture hall. The average class size at a community college is normally much smaller. Even the largest classes at a community college are not likely to have more than 35 to 40 students, the average being around 25. This increases the likelihood of more frequent interaction between students and the faculty member, the ability of the faculty member to better know students and how they learn, and the availability of more one-on-one contact and assistance from faculty.

Mellow and Heelan (2008), in their extensive study of American community colleges, state, "Community colleges dream of perfecting the practice of great teaching so that every student succeeds" (p. 101). The authors claim that the profound diversity at community colleges calls for a very different pedagogy: "one that engages hearts and minds as well as provides the intellectual tools to overcome past educational missteps" (p. 101). They conclude: "Community college faculty are ideally suited to become experts in the scholarship of teaching, modeling for all of higher education the best educational practices for the critical first two years" (p. 101).

Economic factors. The case for studying good teaching and learning at community colleges is strengthened when you consider how many students they enroll, how diverse their student population has become, and how economically efficient they are both for transfer and occupational students.

Community college enrollments are swelling in today's economic climate, increasing by nearly twice the rate of public four-year colleges in the late 1990s (Phillipe & Patton, 2000). Many students who originally planned to attend a four-year university are now taking their first two years at a community college to save money. Nearly half of all community college students receive financial aid.

Lower tuition. According to the College Board's *Trends in College Pricing* (2011), average tuition and fees are $28,500 at private four-year colleges and universities, $8,244 at public four-year colleges and universities, and $2,963 at public two-year colleges. Thus, the average cost of tuition and fees at public two-year colleges is typically one third that of in-state tuition and fees at public four-year colleges, and approximately *one tenth* of the tuition and fees at private four-year colleges.

Workforce increasing educational needs. There has never been a brighter spotlight on community colleges than today, as evidenced by President Obama's remarks:

> ...we know that in the coming years, jobs requiring at least an associate degree are projected to grow twice as fast as jobs

requiring no college experience. We will not fill those jobs—or even keep those jobs here in America—without the training offered by community colleges. (Obama, 2009)

In addition to the increase in community college enrollments and the diversity of students in those colleges, economic factors are crucial. To a large extent, our economic future depends on how well we educate our community college students. Twenty years ago, community colleges were places for less academically inclined students to gain the credentials they needed for a decent job, or for workers driven out of manufacturing positions to re-train for emerging sectors and industries. Today, many of those sectors are experiencing brutal competition from abroad.

Due to changes in the workforce and an increase in demand for two-year career programs, it is clear that not everyone needs a bachelor's degree. In fact, in the future there may be even more jobs for community college degree and certificate holders. But, for these workers to get ahead and to succeed in life, merely training them in new skills is no longer enough. They need to be able to learn continuously, to think critically, and to adapt to a changing economy. In other words, we now need community colleges to impart the same kinds of sophisticated learning and thinking skills that have traditionally been the province of four-year colleges.

The New Normal: Community Colleges Students Today

A recent U. S. Department of Education analysis (Adelman, 2005) shows that as of 2001 nearly two fifths of traditional-age stu-dents (18 to 24) began their college education at the community college; three fifths of students over the age of 24 started college at the community college. The average age of the community college students hovers at around 29; approximately 40% are of "traditional" college age (21 years or younger), but another 40% are between the ages of 22 and 39 (American Association of Community Colleges (AACC), 2006). Two groups of minority students are more likely to begin college at the two-year level: Hispanics and Native Americans.

An increasingly large proportion of college students complete the equivalency of their freshman and sophomore requirements at community colleges. This trend alone is critical to understanding the importance of the teaching and learning experiences for students at the community college level; their first and often lasting impression of college teaching occurs in community colleges. For many students, their first opportunity to become engaged and excited about learning occurs in community college classrooms. And, their expectations, habits, and motivation as learners are shaped by their experiences with the faculty members at community colleges.

All of these factors that describe today's community college students makes teaching in a community college increasingly challenging. Community colleges are different and unique institutions; they are not lesser versions of universities. In fact, teaching practices at community colleges are being studied, because of beliefs that "their faculties will take the lead in developing distinctive pedagogies for the new populations of learners who attend American's colleges" (Mellow & Heelan, 2008). Community college teachers in The Engaged Teacher Study frequently describe the environment they teach in as summarized by this teacher:

> Community college students typically take too many classes, struggle economically to make ends meet, work too many hours, and valiantly try to juggle family and personal issues that create endless distractions and roadblocks as they pursue their education.

Likewise, here is how Roueche and Roueche (1994) summarize the qualities of community college students:

> More and more of today's entering students are unprepared for the academic reality of the college experience — they are working too many hours, they have too many family responsibilities, they are not focused on the personal and professional goals necessary to persist in an academic environment, they come without support from family and/or friends, and they are "unclear" on what they wish to do with their lives. This increasing 'diversity' creates major difficulties and problems for the community college as a teaching/learning institution and for those faculty and staff who labor mightily to help the institution make good on the promise of the open door. (p. 21)

Summary

Teaching matters more now than ever given the diversity of today's students and the related challenges they pose for teachers. A one-size-fits-all pedagogy does not apply to most college students. Community colleges educate a realistic and microscopic view of today's college students and are uniquely positioned to lead the way in developing pedagogies for higher education's population of learners. In many respects, college teaching today is for the committed teachers willing to take on the challenges that increased diversity in the classroom poses. What we need are teachers to engage today's students in learning and thinking that will prepare them to be nimble learners in today's challenging and changing world.

Author Narrative: Office Hours and Other Miracles

Sometimes, when students have fallen behind or are on the brink of dropping the course, or entirely out of school — for whatever reasons — I get the desperate "cry-for-help" email or call. That is when I say, "You need to come see me during my office hours."

If the student does come, I can usually find way to salvage some learning from the course. That doesn't always mean that the student will pass. It all depends on the student. I leave that decision up to them as I lay the cards out on the table.

When a student comes to see me about falling behind in a course, I give them specific assignments based on the work missed. I make this as detailed as possible, but stress that doing the work it takes to stay in the course is up to the effort they put forth. I'm flexible; I'll meet with a student at their convenience. But the student must show up. Like Woody Allen said, "Ninety percent of success is showing up!"

One winter semester, I had a student I'll call "Crystal," who sent me one of those desperate emails near the end of the semester. Crystal had some attendance and homework issues: she had missed two class sessions and had turned in homework late several times. Her participation in class was good and her speeches were average, but her attendance and late work issues were pushing her into the fail zone. I'd been giving her timely feedback urging her to get back on track and see how she could still be successful in the course, as this was her first experience with college.

Crystal, in her late 20s, exuded eagerness and hunger for acceptance from her classmates, and from me. She was always dashing into class right at the last minute, disheveled and breathless. She would race into the classroom and noisily unpack her book bag. Even before I was aware of her unique background, I felt like she added a great deal to the diverse mix of students in the particular class she was in.

Talk about diversity! Community colleges are noted for diversity that reflects the communities they serve, but this class was far more diverse than any of my other classes. The students represented a variety of ethnic and age groups. Plus, I had a home-schooled high school student, a 30-something autistic male student, and another 30-something female student — a mom with an autistic son. A few were Honors students in transfer programs. Another student was an ex-con recently released from a state prison.

As for Crystal, she had spent the last two years homeless, drifting from place to place, state to state. She bravely tackled this topic for her diversity speech, detailing how relationship and financial issues had led her to a life on the streets. The students and I were riveted as she talked about crashing on friends' couches and living in various homeless shelters. There were a lot of questions after Crystal gave her speech, and she handled them well. We could all tell she was proud to have given a speech about this difficult topic and trying period in her life.

The next week she missed class and her homework assignment. The following week she missed class, and a speech assignment. The third week, three days before class, I received an email from Crystal, desperate to find out "what she needed to do to stay in the class." I was in my office at the time and asked her to call me. She did.

"Crystal! Hi, I'm glad you called . . . how are you?"

"Um, okay, I mean okay, but not in school... I'm sorry I missed class, and I know my group met already, but I want to stay in the class and make up the work... I have to drop my other classes, but I want to keep this one. It's my favorite class, and I'm not so freaked out anymore about public speaking... I have my homework assignments done, and well, I really want to get back in my group and work on the final presentation... I didn't have internet service for awhile, with the power being out from the storm and all [this was true, the area had been hit with a storm and without power for a time], I know I'm behind on my group research and all but... is there anyway I can stay in the class?"

I paused and assessed what I was hearing. I thought she was earnest. She wasn't full of outrageous excuses. This was her first semester in college and she lacked some of the skills necessary to be successful. Yet, she seemed hungry for knowledge, skills and bettering herself. She wanted to earn a degree and become a substance abuse counselor.

I decided to let Crystal come back to class, but only if she could pull her weight with the research for her topic and bring it to me in person in a few days. I specified conditions for what she needed to do and when the work had to be completed.

"Okay," I said, "here's the deal: you need to complete the research portion of your group's topic, using the guidelines listed in the syllabus (six to eight sources, a mix of journals, agency web sites, books, recent articles, and a professionally conducted interview with a local expert on the topic). And, bring the source citations and printouts of the articles. Remember, you are responsible for five to seven Power Point slides stemming from your sources, so bring hard copies of those, too. You'll need to bring all of this to my office an hour before class so I can look it over and make sure you're prepared enough to join up with your group. Have you been in touch with them?"

"Well, I haven't been but I will now that you're giving me this break... Thank you so much... I am coming out to the library today and I'll get started... You don't know how much this means to me to have another chance in your class... I really want to do well... Thanks so, so, so much... So, I will see you Monday at one, okay?"

I wasn't sure when we hung up whether or not I'd see Crystal on Monday, but I was sure hoping I would. I could have dropped her, based on my course policy, but I leave a clause about "at the instructor's discretion" in my syllabi so I have some flexibility if a student runs into dire circumstances or just needs another chance. Even after years and years of teaching and excuses, instructors never know for sure whether to bend or stand firm. It is a judgment call and instructors handle it differently, and that's their prerogative. Many times we're disappointed that a student has to drop out, or doesn't try, or has major life events that get in the way—and, sometimes we're surprised.

Crystal surprised me. She showed up on Monday earlier than I had expected her.

"Hi!" she exclaimed as she nearly bounced into my office, purse, book bag, and scrambled folders in tow. She was grinning from ear to ear.

"Crystal, so good to see you! I'm glad you made it."

"I was lucky and got a close parking spot. There's hardly ever nearby spots this time of day!"

"Well... tell me..."

Crystal bobbed back and forth saying, "Thank you, thank you, thank you, I can't thank you enough! I would never have done all of these if I hadn't talked to you and gotten another chance, and I learned so much! I can't believe how much I learned! Look at this."

And on and on it went for nearly 45 minutes. Crystal was on fire! This was no fake act for the instructor; this was real. Her excitement was sincere. Her passion was genuine. Most importantly, she was learning and it was real to her. The learning light bulb had gone on for her, and it was burning brightly.

I smiled and listened, offering feedback and comments. I gave her some additional suggestions. I was truly impressed with the breadth and depth of the research she'd completed, and knew it would fit beautifully with what her group members were doing. In fact, I knew they'd be impressed, too.

Crystal pulled through and she was learning not only what she needed for the group presentation, but more importantly, she was learning how to be a student and take charge of her own learning.

Reflect and respond. As you picture the students you teach in your own mind, consider the following questions and reflect:

• What have you learned from your students, and, how have they influenced your development as a teacher?

- Describe your "best" and "worst" students, and what you learned from them.
- What are the strengths and insights you've developed as a teacher that help you engage today's students in significant learning?

Engaged Teaching Strategy 2a: Mini Interviews

Directions: To acquaint students with each other and discover the diversity in the classroom, pair students early in the semester (if possible, on the first day of class) and instruct them to "interview" each other. Possible questions include:
- Why are you taking this class?
- What is the first television show you remember watching?
- If you could have lived during any historical period, what would it be and why?
- Describe your unusual trait or ability.
- What is it about your background or family that interests others?

After a few minutes of swapping information based on the questions, have students introduce each other, sharing the most interesting things they learned about each other.

Expanded Engaged Teaching Strategy 2b: Creating a Productive Classroom

Directions: Pose the following to students and have them write their responses for a few minutes: "Describe the positive learning experiences you've had, situations where you enjoyed learning and learned a lot, and/or motivating classes you've been in." Ask students to pair up and share their responses with a partner. Then, ask volunteers to share their responses with the large group. Reinforce any concepts, assignments, or teaching and learning strategies which you may have already addressed or used.

Review the list and ask students to form small groups of four to five students they have *not* partnered or worked with yet in the class. Give the groups 8 to 10 minutes to revisit the list and select the top two ideas they would most like to see incorporated into the class. When groups report out, ask them to elaborate on how the idea(s) would work to enhance learning. Conclude by reacting to their feedback and how you will use it in future classes.

This exercise can be adapted to form classroom guidelines or a code of classroom ethics. See Appendix D for a sample Student Code of Ethical Classroom Conduct.

Chapter Three

The Engaged Teaching and Learning Model

Simply put, the greater the student's involvement or engagement in academic work... the greater his or her level of knowledge acquisition and general cognitive development.
— Pascarelli and Terezini

Learning is not a spectator sport.
— Chickering and Gamson

Author Narrative: That Awful First Day of Class

One of my first college classes as a freshman at a mid-sized state university was an introductory sociology class. The first day of class had the same routine: introduce yourself and listen to the professor talk about the course. I was nervous about that whole routine since almost all of the other students were from the Detroit area or Grand Rapids. I was rapidly learning a whole lot more about the major metropolitan areas of Michigan. I had no idea there were so many different suburbs in the Detroit area alone. It was a little difficult to describe where I was from because I grew up on a farm out in the country miles from a major city. My address and school district were two different towns, and no one I met had heard of either one. So, I would briefly explain where I was from while I observed blank stares from my classmates. Everyone else seemed to know where everyone else was from. They all had things to talk about with each other. I listened a lot. "Oh well, I'd blend in somehow," or so I thought.

The moment my sociology professor walked in the room you could tell he was cool. He had long hair, a beard, jeans, and sandals. The other students glanced at each other with unspoken relief over getting a hip instructor. I don't even remember him bringing a book or handouts with him. He just rapped with us for about 10 minutes and then shifted into student introductions. He told us he was from California, which was cool, very cool. Then, he asked us to go around the room and share our names and where we were from. Before we began, he told us about the introductions from the previous class. That's when I began to wish I could disappear.

The instructor laughed as he described how a student from the previous class had introduced herself. "She held her hand up high like this," he said. He dramatically darted his hand up head-high and continued. "Then, she pointed to a spot on her hand at the base of her thumb (he pointed to the spot as he spoke) and said she was from a little town in the Thumb of Michigan (he emphasized the word "thumb") called Bad Axe!"

As he said the name of the town, he got even louder and slower. Everyone laughed. He elaborately illustrated all of this with obvious glee. His attitude of superiority and condescension was impossible to miss.

At that moment, I knew three things: I didn't want to introduce myself, I wished I was invisible, and I was not cool. Not a great way to start my college experience. I sat there dreading the moment the introductions got around to me. I nervously listened to student after student state their name and the familiar suburb or city they were from. What was I going to say? The problem was . . . I was also from the Thumb, but from a much smaller, lesser known area. There was no way I could tell the class where I was from. And there was no way I was going to make any reference to being from the Thumb! Okay, I thought, I'll think of something. I sat quietly in my seat and anxiously counted down the seconds until it was my turn.

I could feel the beads of sweat slowly trickling down the middle of my back. "Oh, why did I wear a white shirt?" I sat there squirming, hoping no one would notice my inner discomfort. "How on earth was I going to stay composed?" I was disintegrating into a muddled mess right there in a classroom on the first day of class. "What was I doing there?" Every insecurity I'd ever experienced erupted in my mind as I tried to focus on what I was going to say.

"Next," I heard the professor say.

"Damn," I thought to myself. It was now my turn to introduce myself. I glanced around the room furtively. There was no way out. I focused my gaze on an electric switch plate cover in the corner of the room and said, "My name is Nan Vader and I'm from Bay City."

There it was. Done. Over. I would now begin my journey from a different perspective and let go of the past I was trying to forget: the small town school, the farm, acres and acres of loneliness, the high school boyfriend who wanted to settle down and get married, sewing all my own clothes, working in the crops, living in the middle of a farm field. No one really needed to know, did they? After all, the first few friends I'd met in the dorm didn't seem at all interested in what growing up on a farm out in the middle of nowhere was like. Everyone in my dorm was interested in meeting President Ford's niece from Grand Rapids. (She was living on the third floor). That was interesting. That was cool.

The professor paid me little attention throughout the rest of the semester. I'm sure that was in part a reflection of how little I spoke up in class. I was intimidated on the first day of class and never fully recovered from that feeling. For the most part, I remained quiet, even when I wanted to ask questions or contribute to the discussions in class.

I was really glad to be in college, but felt under prepared and naive. So, I worked harder and harder to fit in and figure out what was going on. I did well in my classes, taking full advantage of the study and review sessions offered by the teaching assistants. I went to see my professors during office hours and asked the questions I was afraid to ask in class. I tried to figure out what to do.

When I had what I thought was a really good teacher, I tried to sign up for as many classes as possible from that teacher. I'm sure that those good teachers influenced my goals and what I decided to major in. They took an interest in me and the work I did in class. They made me want to come to class because I felt like they valued what I had to say. They made me want to learn. They expected me to work hard and that was one thing I was good at.

Reflect and respond. Thinking of how you welcome and engage students in the beginning of the semester, reflect and respond to the following questions:

- How do you engage students on the first day of class, and keep them engaged?
- What do you assume about students? About how they learn? About their needs?
- Do you recognize those students who are uncomfortable, intimidated, or apprehensive on the first day? And, if so, how do you approach them?
- Think of a time in a learning situation when you felt intimidated, marginalized, or disconnected. What where the circumstances? How were you treated? What was your response?

What Do We Know About Engaged Teachers?

> Good teaching cannot be equated with technique. It comes from the instructor's relation to subject and students; from the capricious chemistry of it all.
> — Parker Palmer

I have so many questions before I walk into class on the first day of each semester: Who will my students be? What do they do? What are their goals? What things will they need to know and work on in order to be successful in the class? What will the class personality be? What, if anything, have they heard about the class, or about me? Will I be able to learn enough about the students, their prior knowledge, their expectations, and the ways in which they learn in order to engage them in learning, in the content, and with each other?

We all hope to be effective as teachers, but the things we cannot control from semester to semester, year to year, are the changes in students and increased demands for accountability in education. I've been teaching for over 20 years, and I constantly consider what I can do to do a better job with my students. I ask myself, "How can I be more effective in helping students learn?"

Countless reports have addressed the question, "What does it mean to be an effective teacher?" The need to continually raise this question increases as students change and demands increase in higher education. What it means to be a good teacher will become even more important as higher education responds to declining resources, pressures for greater accountability, advances in technology, employer demands, aging faculty, underprepared students, and learner diversity.

The Engaged Teaching and Learning Model

In this chapter, several of the key studies on teaching effectiveness are highlighted. Together, the research and studies on teaching and learning, the perceptions of the students, and the experiences of the exemplary teachers surveyed for The Engaged Teacher Study shape the model that emerged from this study, The Engaged Teaching and Learning Model. Each of the four components of the model is examined in the remaining chapters in this book.

The components of the model—Students, Subject, Scholarship of Teaching and Learning, and Self—drive the practices of Engaged Teaching and Learning. The components contain the things you know and do that inform your teaching practice. The model, much like the Johari Window concept (Luft & Ingham, 1955) that was developed to improve self-awareness and interpersonal understanding, has four quadrants that fluctuate in size throughout a teacher's career.

Keep in mind that the components of The Engaged Teaching and Learning Model are constantly in flux. They are affected by variables in the classroom, in students' and teachers' lives, in the environments and institutions in which we teach, in our subjects and professional fields of study, and in what we know about teaching and learning. The premise for understanding and using the model is that the components are *malleable*—they change, they are influenced by other factors, and they are not totally within our control as teachers. Each quadrant in the Figure 1 model represents a teacher's level of information and energy, which fluctuates throughout one's teaching career. The size of the quadrants can change to reflect their proportion relative to the other components in the model.

Truly engaged teaching and learning integrates all four dimensions. The definition of engaged teaching and learning that emerged from the study and the model is *Engaged teaching and learning is the process in which both teachers and students interact and actively participate in learning that helps them reach their desired goals.*

What you will see from the studies examined in this chapter is that there is no one best way to become an engaged teacher, or one best way to engage students in learning. You will not find recipe-like formulas for success. Despite years of research and quantum leaps in what we now know about how people learn, there is not a universally agreed upon approach to becoming an effective teacher. Engaged teaching must be based on our style and strengths, and geared to the variety of students we teach within the culture of our institutions. And, those students — today's students — comprise the most diverse student body in history in every respect.

Students	**Subject**
Who are they?	How can I make the subject relevant and
What do they know?	important to students?
What do I value and believe about them?	What are the big issues and questions of
How are they experiencing their own	the discipline?
learning?	How do professionals in the discipline
	think?

Engaged Teaching and Learning: The process in which both teachers and students interact and actively participate in learning that helps them reach their desired goals.

Scholarship of Teaching and Learning	**Self**
What do students need to know and	What brought me to teaching and what
do?	keeps me teaching?
In what ways can I actively engage	What are my strengths and habits as a
them in mastering what they need to	teacher?
know/do?	What do I need to change or learn to
How will I measure their learning?	improve student learning?

Figure 1. The Engaged Teaching and Learning Model, with four components of Students, Subject, Scholarship of Teaching and Learning, and Self.

What Do We Know about Effective Teaching?

What do we know about truly good teachers? What does effective teaching look like, and what effect does it have? The field of higher education has made an exhaustive study of teaching effectiveness. But, there are no simple answers or single method to assess the complex phenomenon of effective teaching, nor should there be. No one set of prescribed principles or strategies is presented since teaching methods vary greatly by discipline, by teacher, by student needs, and by the situational nature of teaching itself. Perhaps the most common theme emerging from the literature is that there is no one best way to help students learn.

One of my favorite answers to the question, "What do we know about good teachers and effective teaching?" comes from a passage in Palmer's book, *The Courage to Teach* (1998). Palmer describes what a student said to him when asked to describe her good teachers:

> She could not describe her good teachers because they differed so greatly, one from another. But she could describe her bad teachers because they were all the same: 'Their words float somewhere in front of their faces, like the balloon speech in cartoons.' (p. 11)

With one remarkable image, this student said it all. Bad teachers distance themselves from the subject they are teaching — and, in the process — from their students. Good teachers join self and subject and students in the fabric of life.

Palmer goes on to describe what he believes about good teachers:

> Good teachers possess a capacity for connectedness. They are able to weave a complex web of connections among themselves, their subjects, and their students so that students can learn to weave a world for themselves. The methods used by these weavers vary widely: lectures, Socratic dialogues, laboratory experiments, and collaborative problem solving, creative chaos. The connections made by good teachers are held not in their methods but in their hearts — meaning heart in its ancient sense, as the place where intellect and emotion and spirit and will converge in the human self. (p. 11)

Thinking about the experiences that have shaped your teaching practices in the classroom will help you understand why you do what you do. Further reflection opportunities in this chapter will help you discover how your past experiences as a learner and how your mentors have shaped your principles and practices as a teacher.

Reflect and respond. What do you bring to teaching? To be truly effective as teachers we need to look inward and reflect. How often do we ask ourselves how our insights and experiences drive our practices as teachers? We need to ask ourselves:

- Why am I a teacher?
- Why do I teach what I teach?

Take a few moments now to stop and reflect on the questions. As you reflect, grab a pen and write, type, or somehow record your thoughts. Or, talk out loud, call a colleague and share what you think and ask them what they think, or simply state your thoughts out loud to your partner, your dog, your cat, or your plant. Visualize the answers in your mind in living color, create a cartoon character based on your responses, slip into a Technicolor dream. Say it. Just do it. Reflect. Capture it in some way before you move on.

While reflecting, also ask yourself:

- What do I remember most about my mentors, and/or my best teachers?
- What did they do to influence me?
- What kinds of learning environments did they create?
- How did my past teachers — good and bad — influence how I teach?

You probably noticed some themes that stood out as you answered the questions. Perhaps, like many teachers, you realize how your practice as a teacher is influenced by your mentors.

Many teachers admit that they teach the way they like to be taught to, based on the examples of their mentors or favorite teachers. But the truth is, you cannot teach out of someone else's experience; you can only teach out of your own. As Lamott said in *Bird by Bird* (1995), "the truth of your experience can *only* come through in your own voice" (p. 199).

What the Research Reveals About Teaching and Learning

Much can be learned from the literature and research on teaching and learning. Drawing from research, such as the 50 years of studies on the ways teachers teach and students learn, Chickering and Gamson (1987) articulated the following widely accepted principles in their *Seven Principles for Good Practice in Undergraduate Education*:

1. Good practice encourages student-faculty contact
2. Good practice encourages cooperation among students
3. Good practice encourages active learning
4. Good practice gives prompt feedback
5. Good practice emphasizes time on task
6. Good practice communicates high expectations
7. Good practice respects diverse talents and ways of learning (pp. 3-7)

Chickering and Gamson's (1987) goal was to address the teacher's *how* and not the subject matter of good practice. From their perspective, frequent student-faculty contact in and out of classes is the most important factor in student motivation and involvement, most likely leading to better learning. Their theory of learning is widely quoted:

> Learning is not a spectator sport. Students do not learn much just by sitting in class listening to teachers, memorizing prepackaged assignments, and spitting out answers. They must talk about what they are learning, write about it, relate it to past experiences, apply it to their daily lives. They must make what they learn part of themselves. (p. 3)

Chickering and Gamson (1987) insist that the most powerful force that an instructor can enlist in the task of teaching is the student's desire to learn. They found that the instructor's knowledge about learning and about their students increases the instructor's ability to engage students' natural desire to know and learn. This means that learning about learning and learning about how students learn are essential elements of effective teaching practices.

How we approach teaching and learning may require changes in ourselves in order to help motivate students to learn.

Here is a glimpse at how one teacher in The Engaged Teacher Study created a motivating learning environment:

Teacher Snapshot: Creating a Community of Learners

The crucial ingredient was to create a learning environment in which learners trusted me, as a teacher, and knew that I had their best interests at heart. I sought to develop a personal bond or connection between my students and me. I worked to create a true community of learners in which we were all engaged in reaching mutual goals and in which we genuinely cared about each other and helped each other.

It was important that students knew I did not view the college professor/student relationship in an adversarial manner nor did I seek to demean them or expose their lack of knowledge and skills in an embarrassing manner or create assignments and tests designed to trick them. Honesty, a sense of humor, enthusiasm about learning, compassion, and open communication were essential elements that I sought to demonstrate and model in my classes.

The goal of learning is change. The goal of learning is change, according to Fink in *Creating Significant Learning Experiences* (2003):

> For learning to occur there must be some kind of change in the learner. No change, no learning. And significant learning requires that there be some kind of lasting change that is important in terms of the learner's life." (p. 30)

Related to Fink's focus on change is the recent paradigm shift regarding the way we think about teaching. Barr and Tagg (1995) propose that change needs to begin with a shift from the dominant Instruction Paradigm to a Learning Paradigm so that colleges continuously strive to improve the quality of learning for students. Barr and Tagg assert that the goal for all students becomes not simply access, but success.

Students learning to learn. Exciting and relevant research on how to engage students by tapping into their affective and motivational needs has emerged from the field of psychology.

In *Creating Responsible Learners,* Ridley and Walther (1995) explain how students' basic needs of emotional safety, self-confidence, fun, belonging, power, and freedom determine whether the learner wants or feels able to engage in the learning activity (p. 6).

This knowledge can help teachers and students foster an understanding of learning. It can set the tone for a positive classroom environment where everyone is engaged in the learning process. The classroom is where responsibility as a student must start, according to Ridley and Walther, because in order for them to be successful in school and in the world, students must learn to become self-directed, responsible for their choices, and manage their own learning (p. 7).

Now, even more is known about learning due to new insights from cognitive science as well as from neurological and psychological research on teaching and learning. Learning about learning has exploded. The good news for teachers is that research shows that students are more likely to succeed if they better understand how they learn and are given appropriate choices about their own learning (Weimer, 2002).

At the same time, teachers need to become more transparent to students about their teaching. Teachers ought to be able to explain, "Here's why I do what I do." In doing so, they demonstrate research-based practices, which are purposeful and professional, based on principles and understanding of how cognitive learning processes work. Teachers *and* students need to understand the what, why, and how involved in deep and sustained learning.

Moving students from mastery of superficial knowledge structures to more meaningful ones requires an instructor who understands the learning process and helps students gain greater insight and control over their own learning process.

In *How Learning Works: Seven Research-Based Principles for Smart Teaching* (Ambrose, Bridges, DiPietro, Lovett, and Norman, 2008), the authors distill more than 50 years of teaching and learning research into seven key principles. Understanding the principles leads to better teaching and enhanced learning, they contend. The seven principles are:

- Students' **prior knowledge** can help or hinder learning.
- How students **organize knowledge** influences how they learn and apply what they know.

- Students' **motivation** determines, directs, and sustains what they do to learn.
- To develop **mastery,** students must acquire component skills, practice integrating them, and know when to apply what they have learned.
- Goal-directed **practice** coupled with targeted **feedback** enhances the quality of students' learning.
- Students' current level of **development** interacts with the social, emotional, and intellectual **climate** of the course to impact learning.
- To become **self-directed** learners, students must learn to monitor and adjust their approaches to learning.

Deep, self-directed learning, like critical thinking, is learning that evolves from skill in understanding and assessing how one learns. It is not the doing that causes the learning. Rather, it is the thinking about the doing that causes learning. Therefore, teachers must engage students in the habit of critically thinking, analyzing, and reflecting about their learning. By doing so, students will begin to learn *how* they learn.

What Do Effective Teachers Do?

The proper question is not, 'How can people motivate others?' but rather, 'How can people create the conditions within which others will motivate themselves?'
—Edward Deci

What characteristics do you bring to teaching? How do your students and colleagues see you? What do effective teachers do? Some studies have focused on these questions.

Alfred (1994), in a historiography of effective teaching in higher education, summarizes the faculty characteristics important in effective teaching. Effective teachers
- Are enthusiastic
- Challenge themselves and their students
- Have a professional positive attitude about students' abilities to learn
- Practice ethical professional behavior
- Work collaboratively with colleagues

- Are available and responsive to students
- Create a climate conducive to learning and provide alternative ways of learning
- Are knowledgeable about their profession, disciplines, and learning processes
- Are well prepared, well organized, clear, fair, respectful of students and diverse views and talents (p. 271)

Weimer, in *Improving Your Classroom Teaching* (1993), explored five components of effective instruction that emerged from her examination of the literature and reviews on teaching:
- Enthusiasm
- Preparation and organization
- Ability to stimulate student thought and interest
- Clarity
- Knowledge and love of the content (pp. 6-7)

What the best teachers know and understand. Lists of characteristics are helpful to a degree, but to improve what we do as teachers we need more in-depth snapshots of what truly good teachers do to help students learn. Bain has provided such insights in his book, *What the Best College Teachers Do* (2004). Bain and his associates spent years interviewing, observing, and examining 63 undergraduate and graduate school teachers to identify what the best teachers know and understand about their subject matter and the learning process. The major assertions drawn from Bain's study are:
- The best teachers create a type of natural, critical learning environment that helps engage students in disciplinary thinking and diverse learning experiences.
- Lesson plans and lecture notes matter less than the special way the best teachers comprehend the subject and value human learning. They not only get students' attention but also keep it as they seek learning commitments that start with students rather than the discipline.
- The best teachers know their subjects inside and out — they are accomplished scholars, artists, scientists, and the like — and they also know enough about human learning to motivate, engage and challenge students, and to provoke impassioned responses from students.

- The best teachers measure the quality of teaching by whether students retain the material to such an extent that it influences their thoughts and actions.

Most of all, according to Bain, the best teachers believe two things fervently: *teaching matters* and *students can learn* (pp. 15-21).

What happens in class matters. How often do you analyze what you do in the first few days and weeks of a class? A helpful feature of Bain's research (2004) is the series of examples of what the best teachers do early on in class to emphasize internal motivation and increase students' control over their own education. The following list summarizes some of Bain's conclusions about the things the best teachers do on the first day of class:

- They explain requirements using the vocabulary of promises, not the language of demands. In doing so, they invite students to learn, not command them to do so; they often sound more like "someone inviting colleagues to dinner" rather than "the demeanor of a bailiff summoning someone to court." (p. 36)
- They help students see the connection between the important questions of the course and the questions the student might bring to the course, in order to build a connection between the students' lives and interests and the course.
- They engage students in critical thinking as they emphasize questioning.
- They distinguish between types of learners and recognize how to tailor their appeals to individuals to influence how they approach learning.
- They listen to know their learners and their ambitions to foster intrinsic motivation (p. 36).

The teachers in Bain's study "gave students as much control over their education as possible and displayed both a strong interest in their learners and a faith in their abilities" (p. 35).

Bain found that the best teachers understand and exceed student expectations. They embed skills and knowledge in fascinating assignments and authentic tasks that challenge students to rethink their assumptions and models of reality. They create safe environments in which students try, get feedback, and try again. Bain states, "Teaching is engaging students, engineering an environment in which they learn" (p. 49).

Barkley's (2010) research on motivation and student engagement in learning also supports the importance of designing a dynamic learning environment. Barkley suggests, "Students will retain more if they are using multiple senses to process information and are given regular intervals to participate in a variety of activities that help them make sense of the information" (p. 139).

Here is how one teacher in The Engaged Teacher Study provides a valuable lesson to students on the first day of class about expectations and mistakes in the creative process:

Teacher Snapshot: A Crashing Lesson

"You can't get too attached to glass," was this instructor's opening line to the group of students gathered for the first class of Glass Blowing.

He turned, picked up a large blown glass bowl, carefully waved it in front of students so they could see the details of the art piece, and then released his hold: Crash! Shattered glass pieces splintered and spread across the studio floor like wild fire as shocked and bewildered students scattered back from the mess on the concrete floor.

The instructor waited for the shock and shrieks to subside before he spoke again. Then, he smiled and repeated, "You can't get too attached to glass."

Class had begun.

How Scholarship on Teaching is Changing

Teaching without learning is just talking.
        —Thomas Angelo and Patricia Cross

As stated earlier, the majority of the perceptions gathered for this book came from community college teachers and students. Why look at exemplary teachers in community colleges? Community college scholar and proponent Vaughn (1994) states,

Leading the discussion of changing scholarship concepts should be community college faculty members. Since they have defined their roles as teachers and not researchers, they are uniquely positioned within the higher education community to discuss, define, and fulfill the role of teacher-scholar. (p. 162)

Multifaceted teaching roles. In *A Learning College for the 21st Century* (1997), O'Banion describes an overly demanding, if not downright impossible scenario, for community college faculty:

> Teaching is the one profession that expects so much of its members and requires and pays so little. Teachers are expected to be knowledge experts, assessors, evaluators, managers, data controllers, artists, group facilitators, counselors, information processors, lecturers, problem analysts, problem solvers, coaches, mentors, behavior controllers, and value clarifiers. Their formal education is ill-designed to prepare them for these multiple roles; waiters and airline stewards receive more on-the-job training. (p. 14)

Roueche, Milliron, and Roueche, in *Practical Magic: On the Front Lines of Teaching Excellence* (2003), investigate teaching excellence by examining the perceptions of over 2,000 community college teaching excellence award recipients. Their extensive overview of the research on successful college teaching methods summarizes typologies of best practices in undergraduate education. They conclude that the teaching characteristics most highly correlated with effectiveness fall into three categories: intellectual competencies, motivational attributes, and interpersonal skills.

- Intellectual: how teachers engage students on day one, how they organize information, how they give feedback, how they reign in prior knowledge, how they help learners develop goals, and how they scaffold practice and mastery opportunities for students.
- Motivational: how teachers focus on stimulating the learners' intrinsic motivation in balanced ways that include continual assessment and provide opportunities for personal choice and control.
- Interpersonal: how teachers use what they know about the power of interaction between teachers and learners — and among learners — to promote learning (p. 54).

Roueche and associates do not advocate one specific style or orientation to teaching as superior to others, but they do recommend the following:

- Faculty should get to *know* students and how they approach their own learning.
- Faculty need to take the lead responsibility to *create climates* that lead to improved learning.
- Campuses should promote proactive interest in the scholarship of teaching and learning (pp. 151-153).

They also suggest, "Faculty should regularly enroll in courses at the college, taught by faculty members they admire, first to help them recall what being a student is all about, and second to reinforce some of the critical aspects of student learning . . ." (pp. 151-152).

Shifting from teacher to student-centered learning. Weimer, in *Learner-Centered Teaching* (2002), outlines research-supported ways to engage students in deep learning, known as learner-centered teaching. She suggests faculty increase the decisions students can make about the structure and syllabus of the course, the classroom climate, assignments and assessment. The shift from a teaching-centered to learning-centered focus increases student responsibility for learning without compromising the role of faculty as educational designers. At the same time, faculty do give up some power. In fact, besides involving students in decisions about the course, Weimer claims faculty need to do the following to promote a learning-centered classroom.

- Make content and assignments more interesting and relevant
- Provide frequent and varied forms of feedback and evaluation
- Create a climate of learning in which students share power and responsibility for controlling their learning
- Teach and model self-directed lifelong learning
- Do less telling while students do more discovering

Weimer (2002) states that when she changed the way she taught to place the emphasis and more of the responsibility for learning on the learners, "What happened the rest of that first semester took my breath away" (p. 2).

Finkel, in *Teaching with Your Mouth Shut* (2000), echoes Weimer's "do less telling" approach by suggesting that to be more effective teachers should move away from the model of teaching as telling. Finkel suggests using parables and books, seminar approaches, inquiry-based learning, writing and experiences to provide structure and help students become interested in the subject. Instead of telling students what we want them to know, he suggests that teachers should design experiences for students based on what they need to achieve. Finkel asserts that to be effective a teacher needs three kinds of knowledge: knowledge of the subject matter, knowledge of how the subject matter is best learned, and knowledge of the strengths and weakness of his or her students (p. 108).

As noted by John Dewey nearly 100 years ago (1916), education is not merely a matter of telling and being told. Rather, it is an active and constructive process, which, according to Dewey, was generally violated in practice.

Here is how a community college student in The Engaged Teacher Study describes how his art instructor engages students:

Teacher Snapshot: Teaching Students to See

He was dressed in all black, head to toe: from well-worn leather boots to his trademark felt beret that partially covered his graying hair and shoulder length ponytail. He was a powerful figure, greeting students with a piercing gaze and barely audible voice that you had to strain to hear. Which you did, because you did not want to miss a thing he said from the beginning of that very first class until the end of the semester.

On the first day, he asked us, "Why are you taking this class? What is your favorite color? What is your biggest fear?"

I had several fears, and by having us talk about them on the first day of class, he created a learning environment that encouraged us to conquer them. He gave us a safe yet challenging place for creative work to happen. He taught drawing and painting at the community college, and was known as a tough and challenging instructor. He was all of that and more: he was inspiring. He not only taught us how to draw, he "taught us how to see." What I took away the most was how it was all about life. How we see. How we look at it. How we interpret it. How we portray it. How we live it.

I'll never forget him. His Zen-like teaching style influenced me in ways I am reminded of every day as I, like him, practice the craft of drawing and painting and making art. He told us that he was our "comrade in a common struggle to make art" and that the way to do it was to "show up every day in the studio and do the work." On the last day of class, we all hung around, not wanting to leave the community we helped create. His passion and work ethic are with me with every mark I make.

No one best way of teaching. As McKeachie and Svinicki (2006) conclude in the 12th edition of the classic, *Teaching Tips: Strategies, Research, and Theory for College and University Teachers,* there is no universal best way of teaching. Rather than offering up a set of rules to follow, they suggest a multitude of proven strategies for consideration and modification, based on the changing dynamics of today's students and teaching environments. What works best for one teacher can be dramatically different from what is best for another teacher. To develop as a teacher, they suggest developing well-practiced skills, but also using fresh thinking to analyze why some things work or not in your classes. They advise teachers to work diligently to become better by incorporating research-based teaching and learning practices.

Summary

Faced with today's increasingly diverse study body, and having more knowledge about how people learn, teachers are called upon for more engaging and sophisticated styles of instruction to better develop responsible learners. Although just a few of the major studies on effective teaching were discussed in this chapter, it is clear that definitions of good teaching and ways to become good teachers are supported by some key theories and studies on teaching excellence. Additional resources and key literature on effective teaching are included in Appendix A.

Most of what we know about effective teaching has emerged from studies of what teachers do to help engage students in deep and sustained learning. It's not enough to rely upon just one's own experience as a teacher, or infrequent observations of other teachers. Teaching and learning are complex processes. What *is* clear is that engaged teaching does not depend on inborn gifts or mystical qualities. Rather, it can be learned.

Engaged teaching, as illustrated in The Model of Engaged Teaching and Learning presented earlier in this chapter, evolves from the capacity of teachers to interact with four dimensions: students, subject, self, and the scholarship of teaching and learning—which will be addressed in the subsequent chapters.

Student Snapshot: She Cared about Me and Believed in Me

What made her so different is she took the time to get to know each of her students. Not just their names, but why they were in school and challenges they might have in their lives. She made each student believe their success was her success... each time I had class I felt like I had a cheerleader in my corner. She could easily change her teaching style to fit the student she was working with. I always left class feeling like "she gets me."

Every teacher who made their mark in my life and changed my life did so because they cared. They cared if their students came to class, did well, and grew as individuals.

It is really hard to know what goes on at the home of your students. Maybe you're the first smile they have seen all day, all week. Maybe you're the first person to believe in them. Maybe you're the first person they have spoken to about something that scared them or changed them in some way. Maybe you're the difference maker they needed, the uplift to start them on the right track.

For me a really good teacher cares enough to try, cares enough to listen, cares enough to look at the person from a different perspective and in turn this person is able to grow and be their best, sometimes even against the odds.

Author Narrative: Teaching and Learning is a Two-Way Highway

His name was Jewel. He was 19 years old, just one year out of high school. He had been known at his high school as a track star and a talented musician and dancer. He said he wasn't sure what he wanted to do with his life but he wanted to do something with music as it was his passion.

His attendance was good in my class, but Jewel soon got behind in his assignments and presented me with excuses on a regular basis.

"My printer broke, so I don't have my outline . . . I had to work late at the studio last night... I'll bring the homework next week."

This happened several times. It hurt his grade. By mid-term, Jewel was barely passing the class. So, I talked to him after class one day.

"Jewel, you've missed turning in a lot of the homework and with late grades on your speeches, you're barely passing the class at this point..."

"I know, Nancy, but I want to get caught up and stay in class to do the next assignment with the kids in the schools. I won't be late with anything else... I have a printer now. I've just been super busy teaching dance and with..."

I listened and knew that even as close as he was to not passing the class, I knew Jewel needed to do the next assignment: the community service school storytelling assignment. I wanted to let him do it; I needed to see if he would follow through. I knew the rest of the class wanted Jewel to do the assignment, too.

Jewel was excited about the assignment. I could tell by the energy and hard work he exhibited during group practices in class. When I asked the class what they expected from audience comprised of five-year-olds, Jewel led the discussion. It was clear he knew what little kids liked and how they would respond. He encouraged the rest of this group to become more engaged and animated during the practices.

The day I took the class to the elementary schools to perform the stories, it was clear who the "star" was the moment we arrived: Jewel. He was a kid magnet. As soon as we walked in a classroom, he flashed that winning smile and a big wave, rewarded by a giggly reception from the kids. They loved his "big" Afro that day; he'd super-sized it and stuck a comb in the side. Even before the storytelling began, Jewel mesmerized the kids with his deep voice, towering height, and slapstick comedy antics. He effortlessly moved in and out of voices and characters throughout the storytelling, capturing the imagination of all of us, not just the kids. He was compelling, and I'm not sure he knew it.

When I gave him the grade with comments he earned on the storytelling assignment, he was pleased but eager for more feedback.

"You really think I did a good job?"

"Yes, Jewel, and you were a kid magnet! You had the moves, the voices, the expressions... you won over their little hearts! Obviously, you have a real gift for working with little kids. Did you enjoy it?"

"Oh, yeah, I loved it! I wish I could work with little kids. I wanted to be an elementary music teacher and teach little kids to love music like I do, but people would just think I'm a pervert so I can't do that..."

"Listen, Jewel, if you want to be a music teacher, then you should. No matter what any of us does, somebody is going to think something. Isn't that what you love — music and little kids? And, you're good. I think you'd be a great music teacher."

We talked and talked. This student who walked into my classroom with so much charisma and confidence was scared to death to follow his dream of teaching music. I helped him set up an appointment with a counselor to discuss his transfer options before he left that day.

Jewel followed up on it and transferred to a state university into an elementary education music program the next year. He was starting to take responsibility for his own learning and his own life.

I knew I would miss his smile, energy, and even that name, "Jewel." It was perfect. He was, and he shone brightly. He made me want to be a better teacher.

Reflect and respond. Compare your practices to what you've read about from the literature in this chapter as you reflect on the following questions:

- What are your 'best practices' as a teacher?
- What do you know and use from the literature on the nature of learning in the classroom to help students learn?
- What are some of your successes and failures as a teacher, and what did you learn from them?

Engaged Teaching Strategy 3a: "Ideal" Teacher/Student

Directions: Ask students to brainstorm the characteristic of an ideal college teacher (or student) in small groups for four-five minutes. Then, have them agree upon and rank the top five characteristics of an ideal college teacher/student and report out their list to the class. Create a master list from their responses and use it to discuss expectations and what you will do to meet them.

Note: You can vary this exercise by asking students to do the same for "an ideal college student." Discussion can include what they can do to reach the "ideal." This can be used to prompt student goal setting and expectations for teacher/student roles.

Extended Engaged Teaching Strategy 3b: Change Your Habits, Change Your Learning

Directions: Pass out note cards and instruct students to anonymously write a negative habit they have that impedes their success in college. Collect the cards and let students know you will read each one aloud. While doing so, no attempt should be made to determine who authored the card. With the students, discuss categories of the types of habits identified (time management, attitude, etc.) and write those on the board, noting similarities and differences. After reading each card, rip it up and throw it in the wastebasket. Make a point of reminding students they are in control of changing negative habits and thought patterns, and in doing so, can change their behaviors to lead to success in school. To bring closure to this activity, ask students to pledge to eliminate a negative habit and replace it with a positive one for one month. Writing pledges as affirmations can help drive student change. Revisit pledges in subsequent class sessions and provide positive encouragement to students.

Chapter Four

Listening to Students

If you don't know a student, there's no way to influence him. If you don't know his background, there's no way you are going to get in touch with him. There's no way you're going to influence him if you don't know where he's been.
— Manuel Gomes, Student (Nieto, 2004, p. 107)

Author Narrative: Questioning the Limits

There was much more to making the transition from high school to college than my embarrassment over where I came from; there was a world of difference in the teachers I encountered. I discovered that I loved to learn, I liked being a student, and I did well in the world of higher education. I was attracted to certain types of teachers and soon discovered ways to identify them and sign up for their classes. I expected and respected professionalism, and unknowingly was storing away what I saw modeled in the classroom as standards I was developing for myself as a person.

I gravitated to the teachers that exuded passion when they taught. Sometimes it was unabashed passion and other times it was detached and impersonal, yet passion all the same. You could sense the passion the minute you walked in the classroom. Sometimes the passion was about what they taught. Some teachers were primarily passionate about the very act of teaching. And, I learned the most, especially about myself, from those teachers. I learned best from the teachers who had heart, and weren't afraid to show it, and who challenged the way I think. They made me think, and pushed me to take responsibility for my life and my learning.

Ken Byerly was the first professor in college I encountered who had both heart and passion, and the knowledge and wisdom to make him very, very credible. He was tall and mysterious with a full beard that framed his face and increased his intrigue. His dark, smoky eyes were hidden behind thick lenses. His hair fell over his face as he spoke. He rarely smiled. When he did smile, it was a slow, thoughtful smile often accompanied by soft laughter. Most of the time when he smiled it was because something was true or ironic or idiotic, which made it funny. So, the slow, laughless smile worked and became the standard for most of our class discussions. When he spoke, he looked at you. Then, he would stop talking; that was how he drew you in.

The class was a Humanities class called Personal World Views. It was an interdisciplinary blend of philosophy, sociology, psychology, and theology. One of the books required for the course was Paul Tillich's, *The Courage to Be;* it was a book based on the lectures Tillich delivered at Yale University. Those lectures examined contemporary anxiety, the meaning of life, and the meaning of courage in the history of Western thought.

Professor Byerly stretched our minds using Tillich and other world-renowned thinkers to plop us all into the abyss of inescapable anxiety, anomie, and angst. His lectures literally had me on the edge of my seat as I slipped into a world of questions that occupied my thinking day and night. The questions reawakened raw emotions and encounters I had compartmentalized and left behind. Nineteen years of leaving stuff behind, of sorting emotions into categories, of not naming feelings for fear I'd have to acknowledge them.

Ken Byerly was relentless; he expected much of us because he believed we had so much to give. He gave so much, and he made us believe that we had a lot to give, too. And we did. We wrote, we discussed, and we questioned from 7 to 10 p.m. every Thursday night. The scuffed-up linoleum floor of the classroom became the resting ground for cigarette ashes stamped out by army surplus combat boots, bulging camouflage-print book bags, and countless cans of soda pop leaving wet rings of sugary residue. A large blackboard covered the front wall of the classroom and a dull-looking wood and aluminum desk provided space for Byerly's books, papers, and grade book.

I vividly remember the first class meeting. He came in the classroom quietly and smiled at us and simply said, "Good evening. I'm Ken Byerly."

We all looked at him and then looked around at each other. That was it.

He told us a little about the class and then he took attendance. I don't think he ever asked any of us where we were from. It didn't matter. In his class, we were all on an even playing field. At least that's the tone he set, and we accepted it because it was easier than negotiating differences. Not that we were the same because we weren't at all.

I'm sure I was the youngest student enrolled in the class. It was a 490 level class, usually taken by upper level students. I was a sophomore, 19 years old, and just beginning my second year of college. I learned about the others from listening to them tell their stories as they answered questions, and passionately engaged in class discussions.

On the first night of class, as on every night, Byerly wasted no time in firing out a string of questions snapped at us with his powerful voice, much like that of an evangelical preacher: "What is faith? What does Tillich mean by 'the courage to be'? What does your life mean? Why are you here now?"

I was so transfixed that I forgot to breathe at times. It didn't matter, because what I needed more than air were the questions. I don't think I left with a lot of answers to the questions. But, I left that class with a new sense of self and a heightened desire to ask questions. He taught us how to think, and he taught us how to question.

Reflect and respond. Think about your students and how they enter your classroom, and reflect on the following questions:

- Do you typically ask students what they expect from your course?
- What do you do to make student learning the focus of your classroom?
- What drives the instructional process in your classroom?
- How do you design assignments that develop critical thinking skills?
- How do you create a learning environment that engages students in deep learning?

What Do Students Say About Professors Who Make a Difference?

> Students learn what they care about and remember what they understand.
>
> —E. Erickson

What do college students have to say about truly good teachers, and what they do in the classroom to help them learn? Students should have lots to say, given the fact that students now stay on campus an average of over six years to complete an undergraduate degree.

Do we really know the impact we have on students? Examining more studies, such as Light's study, *Making the Most of College: Students Speak Their Minds* (2001), it is more powerful than we think. Based on student interviews, Light concludes that most professors dramatically underestimate their influence on students' overall development.

Light's longitudinal study at Harvard University asked graduating seniors to think of individual faculty members who had an important impact on them in shaping the way they think about themselves, life, the world around them, or their future. Eighty-nine percent of the students quickly identified a particular professor who had an important impact on them (p. 104).

Here is how the students in Light's study describe the professors who had a major influence on them:
- They effectively helped students change opinions or sharpen an analysis.
- They never told students *what* to think, rather, they worked hard to come up with ways to help students learn *how* to think creatively.
- They shared intellectual responsibility, letting students take some of the responsibility for planning and running academic projects.
- They connected academic ideas with students' lives by helping them make connections between curriculum and their personal values and experiences.
- They engaged all students to participate, even in large classes.

- They taught students how to think like professionals. (pp. 105-120)

Here is how one senior included in Light's study described the impact of professors:

> I learned that time spent in classes where a professor simply goes over and repeats what I have just read, or could easily read in a textbook, is not the best use of time. And that time is so precious. What is most exciting is when a professor helps me understand how people in his field think about topics in his field . . . And it is critical he teach things in class that I really wouldn't learn on my own, reading a textbook at the beach. Frankly, if I could do it on my own, then why should I be here? Especially at these prices. (pp. 119-120)

Students crave interactions with credible instructors who provide a glimpse into the professional world. Brookfield (2006) found that the factors comprising teacher credibility (expertise, experience, rationale, conviction) and authenticity (congruence, disclosure, responsiveness, personhood) are what students value most in teachers.

An example of how a teacher relates authentically to a student on the first day of class appears in the best-selling memoir, *Tuesdays with Morrie* (Albom, 1987). This excerpt illustrates how the author, Albom, as a young student, first encountered the teacher that inspired him with endless life lessons and became his friend for life:

> It is our first day of class together, in the spring of 1976 . . . Only a dozen or so students are there, fumbling with notebooks and syllabi. I tell myself it will not be easy to cut a class this small. Maybe I shouldn't take it.
>
> "Mitchell?" Morrie says, reading from the attendance list.
>
> I raise a hand.
>
> "Do you prefer Mitch? Or is Mitchell better?"
>
> I have never been asked this by a teacher. I do a double take at this guy in his yellow turtleneck and green corduroy pants, the silver hair that falls on his forehead. He is smiling.
>
> "Mitch," I say. "Mitch is what my friends call me."

"Well, Mitch it is then," Morrie says, as if closing a deal. "And, Mitch?"

"Yes?"

"I hope that one day you will think of me as your friend."
(pp. 24-25)

Consider how you present yourself to students and the role you assume with them. Here is how one teacher uses disclosure to build credibility and authenticity:

Teacher Snapshot: Learning is a Journey

I let students know that I jog for exercise and that I've completed a marathon, which seemingly has little to do with the subject I teach. Some students are impressed that their middle-age teacher ran 26.2 miles without stopping! I explain how training for a marathon is similar to succeeding in a course. I discuss how I set goals with a timetable and incrementally increase my mileage. I stress that people don't enter the world with well-developed abilities like the stamina of a marathoner, and that there will be ups and downs to any type of learning. The example helps students realize there are no short cuts. Learning is a continuous journey, not a sprint.

Whatever your approach, know that how you present yourself and relate to your students makes an impression and sets a tone that influences how students view you and learning.

The Engaged Teacher Student Survey

This chapter focuses on what students responding to the Engaged Teacher Survey have to say about truly good teachers. It provides data and Student Snapshots that highlight experiences, comments, and stories from students who responded to the survey.

Methods. Over 200 college students completed the Engaged Teacher Survey, including some recent college graduates. In addition to the surveys, an interactive on-line focus group comprised of currently enrolled college students was used to gather perceptions. Approximately two thirds of the students were community college students and the other one third were university students or graduates.

The students were asked to describe:

- Their truly good teachers
- How good teachers treated and influenced them
- What good teachers do to help them learn in the classroom
- What they remember most about the truly good teachers they've had in their life

Student Responses

The students responding to The Engaged Teacher Survey were generous with their feedback, often giving in-depth descriptions of how teachers engaged them. Students rarely mentioned personality traits of specific faculty members, but frequently mentioned how the best faculty members engaged them, challenged them, and related to them in ways that not only helped them learn, but sometimes left a sustained influence on their lives.

The themes emerging from The Engaged Teacher Study relate to the Student quadrant of The Engaged Teaching and Learning Model (Figure 2). The questions are what teachers need to know about students to better engage them in learning. The degree to which students engage in learning is influenced by how much the teacher knows about them, what they themselves know, and how they learn.

Truly good teachers. The most commonly occurring themes from the 200 students about the truly good teachers they've had

- **Focus on learning.** Good teachers make the class interesting and engaging to help students learn. They use a variety of approaches to relate the subject to the students so they learn. They are clear and organized. They patiently give feedback and encourage students to learn.
- **Care.** Good teachers care about the students. Besides caring about students and their learning, they care about students' needs and they relate the subject to students in interesting ways that reach them and connect with their lives beyond the classroom.
- **Have passion.** Good teachers are passionate, enthusiastic, and energetic about teaching and their subjects. They enjoy teaching and make it enjoyable. They are friendly. Good

teachers are concerned with knowing their students, which helps motivate and encourage students to do their best.

- **Communicate well.** Good teachers explain things well, listen well, and communicate well with students. They take time explaining things to ensure students understand, especially things like grading standards, the syllabus, and course policies. They are interesting to listen to and stimulate discussion. They use humor and welcoming communication skills to encourage students to actively participate in the class.
- **Are available.** Good teachers are available in and out of the classroom to talk, answer questions, give advice, etc. They connect with students one-on-one. They display patience, kindness, and a willingness to do what it takes to help students learn.
- **Connect well.** Good teachers make an effort to connect with students and help students connect with the subject by relating it to their lives. In doing so, they gain respect from students. They enhance their credibility by getting the students to think about how the subject connects with their lives. They are authentic.

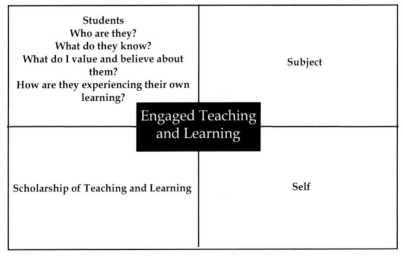

Figure 2. The Engaged Teaching and Learning Model with emphasis on the Student quadrant and key questions teachers need to know about their students to engage them in learning.

- **Challenge.** Good teachers challenge students to think critically, question assumptions, tackle important questions about the discipline, and embrace the big questions about life.
- **Respectful.** Good teachers are respectful toward students, even when students are not respectful to them. They are professional and responsible.
- **Fair.** Good teachers are fair, open-minded, and do not have favorites in class. They treat students as equals and grade fairly.
- **Knowledge.** Good teachers are knowledgeable about their subject and about ways students learn. Their knowledge includes real life experience that helps students understand and apply what they are learning to their lives, goals, and career fields.

The comments of students typically fell into two main categories: how teachers treated students and what teachers did in the classroom to engage students in learning. Below is a sampling of common responses from students.

How good teachers treat and influence students. The most commonly cited qualities were respectful, concerned, supportive, fair, and inspiring. One student commented, "My best teacher believed I had the potential to go far, and still inspires me to this day."

Several students mentioned that the good teachers welcomed questions and taught them to look at things differently. They encouraged students to debate, analyze contrary opinions, and develop critical thinking skills. In addition, they connected with students on a human level, as one student described: "I really love how my teacher got on a human level with the students. She didn't act like we were just another paycheck, but as if we were indeed human."

Many students explain how the way they were treated by teachers influenced their desire to learn and succeed. A returning adult student said:

> My best teachers treated me as though I mattered. My thoughts and experiences were valued, and I was even encouraged, as a non-traditional student, to share some of my life experiences when relevant to the subject of study. I also felt a

level of respect for what I brought to the class, which almost acted as personal accountability to be the best student and a positive role model.

What good teachers do in the classroom to help students learn. When asked to provide more details about specific classroom practices that help them learn, students described a variety of approaches good teachers use to motivate students, frequently describing how good teachers made learning relevant to their lives. Students said the thing that helped them the most were active, encouraging, relevant, and challenging learning environments orchestrated by a motivating and interesting instructor.

Over and over, students described their best teachers as engaging, effective communicators who respected and truly cared about them as students; as passionate and enthusiastic experts in their fields; and as good listeners.

One community college student commented, "Students can tell when a teacher likes their job. You either come in everyday smiling and upbeat, or you don't. It's as simple as that. A good teacher is one that loves what they do, and show it."

An adult community college student, in describing his best teachers, illustrates in detail how two very different teachers can have similar impact.

Student Snapshot: Two
Very Different Teachers Helped Me Learn

When asked about my best teacher, I had two teachers in mind. One had a no nonsense teaching method, and his explanations were clear and easy to understand. He kept the class alert, and attentive . . . . he held my attention, and taught me fascinating things.

The other teacher was less demanding, but was constantly teaching. He taught not just lessons about the material being covered but also taught about life in the working world. The tasks he assigned pushed students to aspire to more than just a grade. He pushed students to be community responsible, and to be great team members whether leading or supporting the leader. In his lectures he helped us see how what we were learning had real life applications.

Both teachers taught subjects that fascinated me. Both teachers took pains to make sure that I understood that they were available if there was something I did not understand. They fed my desire to learn, albeit in different ways. The challenging teacher challenged me to stay focused. The other teacher put me in a team-oriented environment that forced me to learn about others, and my own personal weaknesses.

Both teachers treated all students with respect, and I found them credible. Competence, relevance, and rigor help me learn. To me, the teacher that excelled gave his students projects that he thought would make us better people. He used service projects related to this goal as a way to reinforce the course material. I continue to utilize the things I learned from him. For me, a truly good teacher will keep students involved in the active learning process by helping each student see how the course material applies to real life.

Most students cite active learning approaches when describing how they learn best. Fifty-five percent of the students indicate they learn best by hands-on approaches. A fifth of the students indicate they learn best visually. Combined, this means 75% of the students describe themselves as hands-on or visual learners. The remaining 25% say they learn best by reading, repetition, or memorization. Overall, the majority of the students said they value approaches that give them opportunities to apply what they are learning.

What engaged teachers do and the effect on students. Do students shy away from instructors or courses they've heard are difficult or challenging? It appears not, as students indicate that they prefer and learn more from faculty who create active learning environments that spur student engagement, growth, and success in college. One community college transfer student said that his "best professors are unconcerned with a course being 'too hard' or 'too easy,' but appropriate for the given circumstances."

Students often develop different perspectives of their challenging experiences with teachers over time, as explained by this student who has been out of school for over 20 years.

Student Snapshot: My Best Teacher was Not My Favorite Teacher

My best college professor was definitely not one of my favorites . . . she was an older, tough, no nonsense type of a woman. I was terrified of her, but boy did I learn! She taught introductory English, a subject I thought I was pretty good at. She quickly cleared that thought from my mind. She proceeded to pick apart every piece of writing I turned in. I dreaded her class, but so did every one of her students.

I remember being overwhelmed with an assignment. Past experience had taught me that going to the professor, pleading ignorance, and being charming would most often end up with a better grade and being spoon fed the material. I screwed up enough courage to go see her, expecting the same. Not so. She sat and listened to my sob story, blinking without any other facial expression. She pulled out the lesson notes and asked me if I understood the intent of the assignment. Then she told me she expected me to get it done and on time — then sent me out to do it. And I did. Her firm belief that her students would learn and do well left me no other choice.

She set high expectations for us, which she laid out clearly at the beginning of the year. She stuck with her outline, never deviating from her plan. She graded us all equally and based her grades on what she had already told us she expected. If we didn't meet her expectations, we did it again until we got it right. Her feedback was specific and plentiful.

It was clear that she thought mastery of the English language was one of the most important pursuits we would ever follow, and she expected us to take it seriously. She insisted on nothing but our best . . . . Gradually I found her assignments an interesting challenge. I could tell I was becoming a better writer ...Whenever I did get a compliment, I knew I really deserved it. . . . I was a frightened freshman who had never experienced someone with such rigid standards and high expectations. But I became a better writer because of her unwillingness to accept anything less. I do a lot of writing in my job, and I think back on her lessons even today when I check over reports for wordiness and punctuation. Whenever I reword a passage or choose a more powerful verb, it is because she felt so strongly about writing [that] she made me into a convert.

Overall, students say engaged teachers make learning interesting, enjoyable, motivating, inspiring, and challenging by using a variety of approaches, such as lectures, field trips, activities, debates, examples, study guides, and hands-on opportunities. Engaging teachers create a delicate tension between motivation and challenge.

As one student says:

My greatest teachers treated me with respect, and care, and always drove me to challenge myself. They gained my trust first by showing me they really cared about me succeeding in the class. They were always prepared to go deeper into the content and to provide more information to clarify things that were unclear.

Their enthusiasm and obvious devotion to the subject and teaching itself was contagious and motivated me.

Here is another example of a student's conclusion about good teachers:

My best teachers noticed me... they asked me what I was going into, what I was interested in, if I needed any help. That really means a lot to a student that doesn't have a clear idea on where his life will end up. My best teachers inspired me to not only to look at the book, but look at the world and what's happening around me. I notice things I would never have considered before.

Many students commented that they've only had one or two teachers that they remember as having a big impact on their lives. For some students, it was a teacher who took them out of their comfort zone in ways that helped instill confidence. A university student explains:

Student Snapshot: Goodbye Comfort Zone, Hello Learning!

The moment I knew this teacher was on my level is when she took me out of my comfort zone and had me look at things from a different perspective. From the first day of class, she made everyone feel comfortable—not judged—but, free from ridicule. In her class I had my change of life experience. I did because I knew in the brief time in the class, I had someone who believed in me. That is what makes a teacher a really good teacher—their belief in you, when you don't believe in yourself. Her belief in me, her trustworthiness, and credibility saw me though hard times.

When describing their best teachers, students consistently talked about teachers who were able to bring out the best in them. Engaged teachers have *insight* into what motivates students and they want them to be as successful as possible. In other words, they care.

One student summarized the effect his best teacher had on him as student: "He made me want to be a better student and person."

Great teachers understand and *believe* that if teachers have high expectations about what students can accomplish, they are more likely to treat and teach students in ways that help facilitate course mastery. Consequently, through the *practices* of these teachers, students may achieve more than they believe possible initially.

Reflect and respond. How we treat students is related to how well they learn. As teachers, we communicate our beliefs about our subject, ourselves, our teaching practice, and our students by the way we treat them, shaping what and how they learn.

How do you measure up? Return to the questions in this chapter and reflect on moments in your classroom when you believed students were truly engaged in learning.

As you review what students have to say in this chapter, compare their remarks to how you responded earlier in this chapter about how you treat them and consider these questions:

- How do you treat your students?
- Think back to a class that went particularly well, and describe what you and the students were doing.
- Think back to a class that didn't work. What went wrong? What did you learn and how did you change what you were doing for future classes?
- How many of your practices as a teacher do you see in the students' descriptions of good teachers in this chapter?

Summary

Students see truly good teachers as those who believe in them, know how to relate to them and help them, challenge them, and create opportunities for meaningful learning. These teachers demonstrate credibility, authenticity, and competence while communicating an attitude of respect and caring. Students describe these teachers motivating and engaging them, and often inspiring them in ways that have sustained influence in their lives.

Author Narrative: He was My Hero

There aren't too many instructors I remember vividly, but Professor Byerly is one college instructor that I remember as if I'd just stepped out of his class. What I remember most is how he taught me how to question, how to think critically, and how to go beyond the obvious things in life. I've never stopped asking questions since the night in class 30 years ago when he stunned me by reading my paper aloud.

He walked into class that night and said, "I want to read one of the papers you turned in last week. Existentialism isn't easy to write about, and this student made some important connections. Please, listen."

Then he read part of my paper. I'm not sure, but I think I stopped breathing while he was reading. I was both stunned and proud as I listened. I could barely contain myself as he read aloud. I was so relieved he didn't tell the class it was my paper. Here is part of that paper he read:

> Walking along the beach. Sand squishing between my toes. Wishing I were dead. Wanting to feel alive. Wanting to have my cake and eat it, too. Stuck in the middle of two desires: afraid to let go of the past and wanting to embrace the future. Anomie. Anxiety. I have so many questions: Why me here now? What next? The lukewarm water caressing my bare feet comforts me and makes me feel safe, protected. The prints my feet leave in the wet sand confirm I exist. At least for a while, until another tide comes in and washes away the impressions in the sand, destroying any evidence I exist.

I could hardly wait for class to end so I could get my paper from him and read his comments. I was never the same after that class. So many things changed. I changed. And, I learned so much that I still think about to this very day.

Reflect and respond. Consider the following questions from the Student quadrant of The Engaged Teaching and Learning Model:

- Who are my students and what do they know?
- What do I value and believe about them?
- How are they experiencing their own learning?

Engaged Teaching Strategy 4a: Pro or Con Switch

Directions: Pose a controversial subject-related question and ask students to take a stance — either Pro or Con — and write the word "Pro" or "Con" on one side of a notecard or sheet of paper, depending on their stance. On the opposite side of the paper/notecard, instruct students to write a few sentences supporting or explaining their position. Collect and redistribute the Pro or Con papers to students, making sure they get the stance opposite from their original one. Pair students with opposite reassigned stances and have them explain their new stance as if it were their own. Ask students to report out how this exercise challenged their original thoughts and helped them think differently.

Expanded Engaged Teaching Strategy 4b: Pro or Con Stand-Up Debate

Directions: Pose a controversial question or issue from your discipline and ask students to take a stance (pro, con, or undecided) and write it on a notecard along with a few sentences supporting their position. Have the students stand up and line up according to their position, starting with pro on one side of the room, con on the other, and undecided in the middle. Ask for volunteers to speak, one at a time, indicating that all students will get a chance to speak. After a student speaks, anyone can change their position and move to a different spot on the pro-con continuum to reflect a change in their stance. Continue until all students have had a chance to speak at least once. Debrief by asking for student feedback on how the exercise stimulated them to think about the issue.

Part Two

Engaged Teachers Meet Today's Challenges

Chapter Five

Creating Connections

The purpose of teaching is to help students make passionate
connections to learning.
— Terry O'Banion

If the learning that students are asked to undertake seems
to have no purpose or connection to their own interests and
concerns, they will resist it.
— Stephen Brookfield

Author Narrative: The Seminar that Opened Doors

It seemed like he didn't put much effort into actively teaching
us in his graduate seminar. His seminar, or "Dr. W's Seminar"
as it was commonly called, was required in the program, and it
was the only class he actually taught. He chaired the program as
well as most of the dissertation committees. As first year doctoral
students, we were all in frequent contact with him. A few of the
students, myself included, were graduate assistants in his department. Students looked forward to taking his seminar, given
he was the head of the department and nationally renowned
for creating the state plan for community colleges in the state
of Florida. His cohorts and students affectionately knew him as
the "Father of the Florida Community College System." Since
he was the chair of most of our dissertation committees, we had
hopes of co-writing an article with him after we completed our
PhDs; many of us did.

Here is how his seminar went: Each week Dr. W. brought in
a guest speaker, such as a college president or executive-level
administrator, a school superintendent, or a legislator serving

on key education committees. It was an impressive line-up for our first semester of graduate school. Instead of a traditional classroom, we met in the departmental conference room and sat around a large conference table with the guest speaker and Dr. W. sitting at the head of the table. Each class began with our introducing ourselves, saying where we were from, what our positions were (working, full- or part-time graduate student), and what our dissertation topics were. After the seminar was over, we all walked up to the head of the table and thanked our guest speaker with a handshake, commenting on something significant we learned from the discussion.

Although Dr. W. simply introduced the speaker and facilitated questions near the end of the seminar, he was in complete charge of choosing guests and their suggested topics. We soon realized that what he was doing was brilliant; not at first, when we wondered if he was ever going to lecture, but certainly by mid-semester when we all knew we were experiencing something special in his seminar. The value of the seminar became apparent as we neared completion of the program and sought career opportunities: we knew most of the community college presidents and key leaders in the state education system.

We were required to create and present a final project for the seminar based on what we learned. I didn't know where to begin, as I'd learned a great deal. So much of what the community college presidents had talked about interested me: unique programs at their campuses, their leadership styles, and the origins of the community college movement in the state. I needed to develop a focus and direction for my project, so I made an appointment with Dr. W. I talked to him about what interested me and he replied, "I think you should visit some of the campuses. Just let them know when you're coming. And, you can borrow my camera and take some slides."

Well, that did it. I took his advice to see the state's colleges for myself. I scheduled visits at six or seven campuses, taking his camera loaded with a roll of slide film. I met with the president or a vice president at each campus, many of whom I had met as guest speakers at Dr. W's seminar. When I mentioned that I was a doctoral student of Dr. W., they made it a point to meet with me and were generous with their time and knowledge.

I toured each campus, took pictures and reviewed their programs. It was exciting to see firsthand the system of community colleges — one strategically located in each county in the state — that Dr. W. had decades earlier envisioned in his dissertation. I returned loaded with notes, impressions, and information . . . and several roles of slide film to be developed.

My final project for the seminar was a presentation about the strengths of the community college and the educational opportunities it afforded students. At the end, I dimmed the lights and clicked through the images of the colleges I'd visited: their campuses, the people I met and interviewed, the communities where the campuses were located, and the students. When it was over, I turned the lights on and looked to the back of the room where Dr. W. sat quietly, wiping tears from his eyes.

I had learned a great deal with the help of a great teacher.

Reflect and respond. As you continue to read, reflect on these questions.

- What is your teaching philosophy, and how has it changed throughout your journey as a teacher?
- What do you do to make your subject relevant and interesting to your students?
- What are the big issues and questions in your field? How do you engage students to care about and pursue those questions?
- What do you do to introduce your students to the way professionals in your field think?

The Engaged Teacher Study Survey: Teacher Perceptions

To discover what truly good teachers have to say about teaching, 150 award-winning teachers were sent The Engaged Teacher Survey. One hundred teachers responded, a dozen were interviewed, and several were observed in action. What these teachers have to say will be discussed in this chapter and the next two chapters.

The 100 teachers responding to the surveys answered the following questions:

- What is your definition of a good teacher?

- What do you know and understand as a teacher and professional in your field that helps you engage students in learning?
- What questions do you ask yourself when you prepare to teach?
- What do you expect of your students?
- What do you do to create a positive learning environment?
- What do you do when you teach?
- How do you treat your students?
- How do you check your progress and assess your effectiveness?
- What kinds of things do you do out of the classroom that contribute to making you a good teacher?

Teachers responding to the survey spoke repeatedly of the following: passion, responsibility, caring, staying current in their fields, keeping abreast of the scholarship of teaching and learning, active learning, reflective practice, challenge, respect, belief in students' ability to learn, role of the teacher, assessment, helping students make connections, and the need to know how students learn in order to help them learn. Numerous examples of how teachers responding to the survey engage students in learning will be illustrated throughout this chapter.

How Good Teachers Help Students Create Connections

Good teachers employ a variety of approaches to help students create learning connections, including those explored in this chapter: passion for their subject, students and teaching, teaching philosophies, and engaging students through reflection, classroom research, commitment, and trust.

The exemplary teachers surveyed for The Engaged Teacher Study described good teachers as those exuding forms of passion about their subject, students, and teaching. This passion helps connect students to the teacher, subject, other students, and most importantly, to learning. Most of them agreed with this comment from a university teacher:

Great teachers *love* the subject matter they teach and know it well... they love to tell people about that subject matter . . . they desperately want the audience to *understand* what they are telling them. They know the essential issues in their discipline, the questions of their students, and design the course accordingly.

Connections between students, subject, teacher, and learning are illustrated in The Engaged Teaching and Learning Model (Figure 3).

The following questions address knowledge of the subject and teaching strategies:

- How can I make the subject relevant and important to students?
- What are the big issues and questions of the discipline?
- How do professionals in the discipline think?

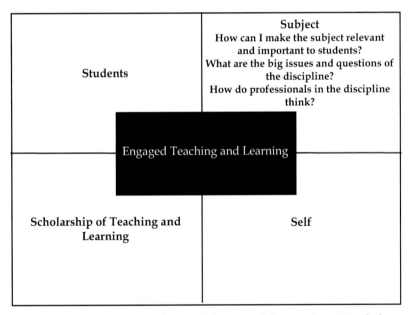

Figure 3. The Engaged Teaching and Learning Model with emphasis on the Subject quadrant and key questions teachers need to ask themselves to help engage students in learning.

Knowledge, Passion, and Personal Teaching Philosophy

A good teacher must have a passion for what they do. Their passion for the subject they teach should only be surpassed by their passion for teaching.
—Scott Miller, Community College Instructor

Have you ever taken the time to write out your teaching philosophy? Perhaps you were asked to articulate it when you interviewed for a teaching position. Some teachers put a brief version of their teaching philosophy in their course syllabi. A teacher responding to The Engaged Teacher Survey explains his teaching philosophy as follows:

> I try to create a learning environment that is emotionally, intellectually, and psychologically safe. I understand that students learn differently. I acknowledge what I don't know to show that I am still learning and that I am still a student. Most importantly, I try to provide them a strong love for continuous and everlasting learning. Encouraging self-reflection is the first step in creating successful students. My primary goal is to inspire my students to be willing to facilitate their own learning so that they will be life-long learners. Caring about my students and what I am presenting is very important to me.

Reflect and respond. If you have not written your teaching philosophy, try this exercise.

Imagine that you are leaving teaching and you only have time to tell or write your students a few keys things before you leave; what would you want to leave for your students to think about? Consider these questions:

- What would you tell them?
- What words of wisdom would you leave to guide their future lives?
- How would you prepare them to continue what you had started?
- What are the things you would want them to continue to do in your absence?
- What do you want them to do and know?

Or, you may just ask yourself, what would I advise my students to do once I am gone and others continue in my absence?

In this chapter, you also will have a chance to think more about how you create connections for your students by discovering the passions, beliefs, and practices of the exemplary teachers surveyed for this book. Thinking about your teaching philosophy is a good way to start to reflect on your teaching practice.

A Teacher Snapshot illustrates what one teacher says to her beginning community college biology students after the first exam. She tries to motivate them by pointing out where they began as learners and what they can achieve with work and help. She does this early in the semester when the uncertain freshman are crying over their poor test scores and wondering how they will ever manage to pass the class. A story she tells encourages her students to accomplish more:

Teacher Snapshot:
Passionately Motivating Students with Shamu

Let me tell you about Shamu, you know, the whale from Sea World. How many of you have been there? Seen Shamu? Know what I'm talking about? Shamu, the killer whale featured in shows at Sea World, is exactly what you need to be all about to do well in this class. This may be the first college science or biology class for some of you, and if it is, I don't want you to get discouraged. You need to understand what it's like to learn something new, and adjust to the time frames it takes to do so, which are built into the structure of this course.

Just like Shamu, instead of leaping 50 feet out of the water on the first jump, you learn how to jump that high by beginning at the bottom, with small jumps. All the while, I'm just like the trainer at Sea World that keeps raising the fish up higher and higher as you learn and build on what you're learning. I promise you that is what I'll do all semester to help you. You have to show up, prepare, put forth the effort, and I'll be here to coach you higher and help you learn. I believe in your ability to learn.

This biology teacher describes a truly good teacher as one who "cares deeply about the students, the subject matter, and the learning process," emphasizing that all three components must be considered during all phases of the teaching and learning process. Her expectations for her students are clear:

> I expect them to be active participants in their own learning process. I expect them to take full advantage of all of the learning opportunities and tools that I make available throughout the semester. I expect them to respect themselves, each other, their instructor and the learning process. I expect them to earn their grade.

She says she treats her students ". . . like the adults they are":

> . . . I try to guide and facilitate their learning without holding their hands or talking down to them. I share the passion I have for learning and knowing that comes naturally to me, and found that 80% of students will respond to that alone. I believe that my students come from all walks of life (age, background, responsibilities, learning capacity, etc.) and that my job is to get the best out of each of them. Teaching is very much like coaching, you need to encourage them to work hard together toward a common goal . . . they all should be able to contribute.

Here is how a community college English professor describes different kinds of passion in teaching. In her description, notice how she describes how teachers use their own passion about subject, students, and teaching to connect with students:

> Truly good teachers have genuine passion for what they do and the disciplines they teach. Teachers can have many personalities (some teachers may be passionate in a rah-rah way, but that is not a requirement of "good" teaching. A quietly reflective teacher with genuine passion will communicate to most students). Students pick up on the authentic teachers and tap into that passion. Some students will follow their instructor's interest in a field or discipline just because that passion resonates. Good teachers love both the discipline they teach, and the students that they teach. It shows. Good teachers never feel they have learned enough, or have gathered all the disciplinary knowledge they need. They are questing all the time for more.

As this teacher says, passion is displayed in many ways. A teacher may be passionate about keeping up in their discipline, providing feedback to students promptly, or about the teaching and learning process. However the passion reveals itself, it influences the teaching practices of the faculty members in ways that enhance learning connections and engage students.

Here is how another teacher describes how his passion helps him connect his subject to student learning:

> I visit elementary and junior high classrooms, trying to fuel the fun of science... I'll talk about my recent dinosaur discoveries or acquisitions... I also *do* my science, not just teach it... I continue to conduct research and publish peer-reviewed papers in geologic journals... several of my students have been co-authors of these presentations as well. I continue to take students on field trips across the country where they can see a lot of geology and give them a chance to dig dinosaurs also. Seeing it first-hand, and digging up bones, is worth so much more than just reading it in a textbook.

Another teacher emphasizes the importance of connecting students with the subject in ways they become involved and interested:

> A good teacher gets out of the way of students learning the intended lesson by not being petty, mean, boring, disorganized, inarticulate, unprepared, or dispassionate. So, a "good" teacher has to be the "uncola" of all those attributes, but also more. A good teacher lays herself on the line—she's honest. No false notes. Students smell that like four-day-old fish. A good teacher knows the subject and is prepared to teach it . . . shows how she has something interesting to share with them [students], some of them may find it passionately interesting like she does, and she finds some niche where students can become involved, feel connected to what she's teaching. Good teachers create that honest, good experience in the classroom and are interested both in subject and students—not fake interest, but actually interested. And this last thing is key—everything may ride on this—a good teacher listens.

Helping Students Make Passionate Connections to Learning

Many teachers in the study mentioned the importance of engaging students in the subject, giving vivid examples of how they connect with students in their classes. According to the vast majority of respondents to The Engaged Teacher Survey, effective teachers do the following:

- Engage students in active learning that is relevant and connects that learning to their real life, whether college or their career
- Know the subjects and know the process of teaching
- Connect with students, reach them at a level that changes them, make them want to be better and learn more
- Awaken and sustain intellectual curiosity in students
- Both challenge and support students
- Reflect on their teaching and do something with the evidence about their teaching in order to improve it

The consensus of award-winning teachers is that a good teacher passionately strives to connect students to the subject and make them aware of their own learning. Good teachers bring an irresistible energy to their work, igniting and motivating students to learn. They are also lifelong learners, always growing as professionals, who bring their experiences into the classroom. Finally, good teachers care about students and want to see them develop and evolve as learners and human beings.

The compassion this teacher brings to his students' learning is obvious in his description of how he treats students:

> I treat all my students equally, with a love and affection... I tell them they are my academic family and they have nothing to fear but fear itself and my satisfaction as teacher will be fulfilled if all of them are successful in the class and if all of them come back years later and show me how successful each one has been in his or her life.

A community college student describes how her teacher connected the passion he had for his subject to students' lives:

Student Snapshot: The Teacher Made Me Want to Learn

I walked into the class dreading the subject. For me, government was always a struggle. I would never think I would be smart enough to receive an A in the course, but I did. From day one in class, he made me want to learn. Government, no less, a required course. I signed up for his government class because the time slot fit into my schedule. I didn't even know what the teacher's name was until I read it on the syllabus. He was passionate about how important government was in our lives, and his excitement was contagious. His passion for government wasn't the only thing he was cared about, he was passionate about many things and he would use real life and interesting examples to help us learn about government. It was intriguing to listen to his stories and then surprising when you found out it was simply to help you learn. It was almost like he tricked you into learning. He was organized and kept the classes lively and flowing, with lots of classroom discussion. He was always asking us questions, and waiting. He was good at relating the course topics to our lives and making it real. He made us question, think, and connect the dots between what we were learning in class and what we were doing in our lives every day. It was like I couldn't shut off the questions in my mind between classes, that's how good he was. He made me want to learn. He made me want to be a better student.

Creating Learning Connections in the Classroom

One of the things that I grappled with early in my teaching career was how to connect my own journey as a learner and professional in ways that engaged my students. I wanted to challenge their linear thinking about school and careers to illustrate the paths available to achieving their goals and dreams. I decided to use my passion for lifelong learning and change to illustrate the connections to what I teach, given my own diverse background as a student.

Over the years I've developed a way of introducing myself to my students that piques their interest in the subject. I give out a list of possible guest speakers and tell them to look it over and choose two or three persons from the list that they'd like to hear speak during the semester. They do this in groups. I explain to them how to reach consensus on their desired speakers quickly in a group and then give them a time frame to discuss the list and report out their top choices. The list looks like this:

Possible Guest Speakers

Food Service Worker
Professional Nanny
Seamstress/Designer
Copy Writer/Graphic Artist
Career Advisor
Manager
Professor
Small Business Owner
Motivational Speaker
Management Consultant
Law Enforcement Trainer
Focus Group Facilitator
Strategic Planner/Consultant
Health Care Management Trainer
Marathon Runner
Magazine Writer
Pianist
Book Author
Poet
Photographer
Community Volunteer
Wedding Officiate
Missionary
Farmer

The student groups report out their top choices after a few minutes. Among those usually listed as top choices are Professional Nanny, Motivational Speaker, Marathon Runner, Book Author, Photographer, and Community Volunteer. Then, I tell them that over the course of the semester they will in fact have *all* of these "guest speakers" in class because this is a list of all the jobs and experiences I've had in my life. Students are typically surprised and ask related questions.

Part of what I try to convey to them with this activity is that no one is born a speech teacher, engineer, artist or whatever, but rather, that all of our life experiences contribute to who we become and what choices we make. I share with them that I am a first generation college student and understand that for many of them college is a new experience, and perhaps a culture shock.

This introductory exercise is used to prompt discussion of how their own experiences have impacted their lives and how their skills in jobs or experiences are transferable to their career goals. I tell students that I will bring in guest speakers throughout the semester, and I do.

How Teachers Create Engaging Learning Connections for Students

The Engaged Teacher Survey reveals that some teachers bring their experiences and excitement to students in ways that connect directly to what they're learning. Some teachers design community service, research, or field experience opportunities for students to apply their classroom learning in related contexts. Often, students develop their own passion for learning and the field itself through these experiences, particularly when a skilled teacher guides them.

Many of the teachers in this study discussed how they use forms of student reflection to help students make passionate connections to learning. The types of reflection strategies and how teachers incorporated them into their teaching practices varied. Some teachers described using reflection in simple assessment questions, asking students, "What do you think about what you learned?" Other teachers used reflection with writing assignments, discussions, poster boards, analysis papers, and presentations where students actively applied what they were learning in graded assignments. The purpose of most of the reflection strategies was to get students to analyze what and how they were learning. Some of the teachers used reflection activities to understand their students' lives, cultures, and aspirations, as well as their learning goals.

Creating connections through reflection. A unique example of making learning connections using reflection is the last assignment one instructor gives students as part of an exam. They are to write a letter to themselves. The instructor keeps the letters for one year and then mails them to the students. Here's a reply the instructor received from a student after sending him his letter:

Student Snapshot: Do You Remember Me?

Hi, my name is Raul . . . you might not remember me... [because] I enrolled under Roberto... not my real name. I was an illegal alien who wanted to get a better education. . . . The first year was hell. I often had to eat from dumpsters and spent nights in the streets. Things got better and I got a job and a place to live. I lived under an evergrowing lie that kept me dodging authorities one way or the other every single day... I ended up in your class which brings me to the point of my letter. I'm writing this letter because I wanted to thank you for all that I learned in your class. Why? I accidentally found my "Letter to Myself." I read it and was surprised to find out that 90% of what I wrote I would like to do in the next 12 months has been successfully accomplished. In your class I was able to be myself, to learn and to dare. In your class I was not an illegal alien hiding from the border patrol. In your class I could plan and I could err. In your class I felt free. Thank you. One day I got caught. I had to leave the US in pretty much the same way I entered: running. I left everything and everyone behind. But, now I have a job I like. I don't use... any of the programs you taught us. However, I have never stopped shooting for the stars. You taught us that lesson well. Again, thank you. I work for one of Mexico's largest and oldest newspapers... It's a very hectic, very demanding and very challenging job—just like your class, but it's a job I learned how to do before I even knew that I was going to be doing it. Thank you. Please keep teaching your students to shoot for the stars. It really does make a difference.

Creating connections through classroom research. Many teachers in this study expressed the belief that students make important connections through active and reflective involvement in their learning. Some teachers cited the importance of using active classroom research approaches like one-minute papers, pre-knowledge assessments, and feedback surveys (Angelo & Cross, 1993). These practices all help make students more aware of how they are learning and can be used to encourage greater student responsibility for their own learning.

In my own classroom, I desperately want students to take

more responsibility for their own learning, yet at the same time I acknowledge that I cannot control all of the myriad factors and habits students bring with them into the classroom. I believe in students and their ability to assume more responsibility for their own learning if they are given the support and the *resources* to do so, and if they put forth effort.

Sometimes, students are just not interested in taking charge of their own learning, or don't know how. They don't put enough time and energy into their education because conflicting work, family, health, or financial issues hinder them. Sometimes they are just not ready to learn, or they are taking too many credits and working too many hours while balancing personal demands. Some students fail because they don't believe they have the ability to succeed. Thus, they don't try. Instead, they blame failure on lack of talent or intellect, not their lack of effort.

An anonymous survey I ask students to complete in one of my introductory public speaking courses has worked well to raise student awareness and responsibility for their own learning. I adapted some of the items on Angelo and Cross's (1993) Group Instructional Feedback Technique (pp. 334-338) and Brookfield's (2006) Critical Incident Questionnaire (pp. 42-43) in ways that drew out what I wanted to know about how students were experiencing learning in my classroom. I administer the survey, that I call "Mid-Semester Assessment," around the mid point of the semester. I tell the students that I will report how I will be using their feedback to improve learning in the class (and I do in the following class session). The questions and form are included in Appendix B.

A review of some representative samples of student responses reveal how students are experiencing learning in one class and give me feedback for improvements:

What are the things in this class that help you learn?
- The conversational style. By that I mean the feeling of talking "to us" not "at us."
- We do a lot of work together in groups and the way we discuss and communicate.
- Participation of other students helps. Good course content. An engaging teacher.

- When things are well explained. The relaxed, positive atmosphere. Visual aids.
- I like how this class enables free discussion and allows for us all to participate. There's no hostility and this is the one class I feel most connected to for this reason.
- Honestly, the late policy helps me to learn the most. I have already used the 'free late pass' to get it out of the way, thus <u>requiring</u> me to be punctual with my work. I have horrible procrastination habits and in other classes where I can turn work in late I have a habit of accepting the 25% off or whatever, and that is not a good policy at all.

What are the things you do to help yourself learn?
- I take notes, I study, and I practice.
- I use notecards like you suggest. I figure that if I write it down I will remember it.
- I learn best through experiences, personal or otherwise. I learn facts through stories. I take notes at least every paragraph when I read the textbook.
- Listen, pay attention, and finish all my work on time. I also work well in groups.
- To help myself learn, I try to regurgitate what I've learned by using it as quickly as I can by doing it or telling it to someone else. I try to bring it back. Put it to use!
- Listen not just hear the discussion. Try to participate but I felt very nervous and tense. Lack of confidence is to blame.

What specific ideas or suggestions do you have about this class?
- Maybe let the students vote for what speeches they want to give. Like, give a possibility of 8 different speeches and let us vote for 4 out of the 8 types of speeches.
- The community service is great, and you could even try to use more of it.

As you might expect, not all questions elicited helpful feedback, but I do take the results back to the students and subsequently make adjustments based on comments to improve student learning.

With this survey, I discover many things that help and hinder student learning. Also, I revisit issues with the students related to how they help themselves learn: the issues that only they can control.

Although we can't force students to take responsibility for their learning, we can gather information and use what we discover to create deeper learning connections in our classrooms. We can also make students more aware of ways they can take charge of their own learning and create connections to the subject in their lives. We can design teaching approaches to provide pathways to the resources they need to become responsible and engaged learners.

Creating a positive learning environment and providing support that students need can help students make learning connections.

A community college instructor summarizes the principles she follows to raise the bar for student learning:

> I communicate high expectations and my belief to students that they will be successful in meeting those expectations. I think that, if the right environment is created, most students can achieve much more than they think they can. It is my job to create that right environment by being very clear about assignments and encouraging their learning at all times. I think constructive feedback is important and I try to provide it as quickly as possible.

Commitment and connections. For many exemplary teachers responding to The Engaged Teacher Survey, their commitment to student learning is evident in the ways they connect what they are doing in their fields to their role as a teacher. Many teachers shared how they engage in reflection about what they are doing and learning as teachers just as their students do so as learners. Some expressed their deep commitment to students. Here are some of their remarks:

- A good teacher must know the discipline they teach inside and out. This person must keep up with the changes and new discoveries in their discipline. A good teacher must then be able to convey this information to their students in a way that sparks their curiosity and imagination. More importantly though a good teacher must help the students connect this information to their lives. They need to see the usefulness and application of this material or it will be lost.

- A good teacher is one who is constantly aware of and engaged with reflective practice. That is, she considers the assumptions of her discipline, her teaching philosophy, her learning philosophy, her school's culture/mission, and her students' background/goal for education. She doesn't pretend that she or her discipline knows everything, and allows that students are integral and active participants in the *creation* of knowledge.

- From day one, I try to create an environment where students feel safe. College was a scary place for me, and it still is for many students because many are reaching far beyond their comfort zones in order to be there.

Many of the responding teachers say involvement in their field, meaningful self-reflection, and a student-centered teaching philosophy are integral parts of their practices as teachers. Palmer (1998), along with these teachers, asserts that such practices and beliefs do shape the way teachers treat students, which has a significant effect on how well the students do in school. This belief was expressed repeatedly in practices described by the exemplary teachers responding to this study. A veteran teacher put it this way:

Teacher Snapshot: My "Best" Work

A good teacher is generous with his or her knowledge and time. A great teacher inspires the love of learning and giving it back to others. . . . A student asked me, 'What was your best work?' I told him that he was my best work along with all the students that I teach. Yes my work matters . . . but, it's the work of my students that will carry on well after I'm gone. Among my best work are my students who go on to be teachers, giving back the gift of education to the future generations.

Throughout most of the studies on effective teaching, including this one, good teachers repeatedly stated some version of the statement, "Students don't care what you know unless they know that you care."

One of the teachers responding to The Engaged Teacher Survey described how he created connections to students through sincere caring and respectful listening:

> I truly respect each student. It is vital because what a student says is often not what he is really saying. Empathetic, receptive and analytical listening skills are needed. Students come from diverse and often troubling and complicated backgrounds. You have to try to hear what they are saying.

Creating connections through trust. Revisiting Bain's (2004) study, he describes how the best teachers in his study displayed a genuine investment in the students (p. 139). One of the teachers in his study, Jeanette Norden, says, "Our teaching must communicate that we have an investment in the students and that we do what we do because we care about our students as people and as learners" (p. 139).

There are some strongly stated *rules* that the teachers in Bain's study insist upon. The teacher has effectively said, as one of the study subjects puts it, "I will do everything possible to help you learn and develop your abilities, but you must decide if you want to engage in this experience. If you do decide to join this enterprise, there are some things you must resolve to do to make it worthwhile for you and others in the group" (p. 139).

Clearly, the teachers in Bain's study—like the ones in The Engaged Teacher Study—place responsibility for learning both on the teacher and the learner. And, they communicate it strongly to students.

The principles expressed by the teachers in both Bain's study and The Engaged Teacher Study emphasize several forms of connection-building trust: trust in themselves as competent, credible, caring teachers; trust in the teaching/learning process itself; and trust in students. That trust is built on the firm belief that students want to learn, and until proven otherwise, that they can learn. Professors in Bain's study who established this special trust with their students were more likely to experience the following learning connections in their classrooms:

- A kind of openness that encourages sharing their intellectual journeys — joys and frustrations — thus, encouraging students to be reciprocally candid and reflective.

- An open and interactive atmosphere where students ask questions without reproach or embarrassment and where a variety of views are freely discussed.
- Students learn from each other, bringing their experiences and collective insights to the classroom.
- A sense of awe and curiosity about life.
- Students and teachers saw themselves as fellow travelers, students of life, comrades in search of knowledge and truth. (pp. 141-144)

Summary

Good teachers exhibit passion, caring, and self-awareness based on their belief that most students want to learn and that they *can* learn. They also believe that teaching *does* matter, and they help students create significant learning connections through teaching practices and teaching philosophies. Engaged teachers leverage their passion and knowledge to drive practices that help them connect with students and create learning environments that both challenge and encourage student learning and growth. They practice much of what has emerged from major research studies in the field of teaching and learning.

Author Narrative: Passion and Reflection

I was in my fifth year of teaching full-time (at a community college) when I encountered a class full of students who were both a challenge and a blessing. My early morning class was a rich mix of students at various stages and from diverse places. Here is a snapshot of the students in that class: a middle-aged Baptist minister, an exchange student from China, three single moms, a student who grew up in Central America, a reverse transfer student, two honors students, a student athlete, two nursing students, and six first-time college students who ranged in age from 17 to 25.

At the time, I was fairly new to full-time teaching as I'd spent the previous seven years as an independent contract trainer for business, health care, and law enforcement. Based on my experience working with professionals in these fields, I was constantly developing applied assignments and case studies drawn from my consulting work.

My goals in the class were to create learning experiences and assignments for students that they could relate to and use to make connections that were meaningful in their own lives, experiences, and future career aspirations. I used a variety of reflection papers that required students to "do" something (i.e., conduct an interview with a professional, work in a group to problem solve a case study, analyze behaviors in field settings, etc.). Based on what the students did, the reflection papers required them to write an analysis of their experience that synthesized some of the major course concepts into what they learned from the activity or observation they conducted.

Just before mid-term, as the students and I were discussing an upcoming reflection paper assignment, they asked me if the class could go on a field trip. I asked them what they had in mind, and how it would relate to the course. After bouncing around some possibilities, we decided to investigate visiting an area homeless shelter. The students were curious and said that a tour of a homeless shelter would help them "see" some of the issues we were discussing in class.

After a few phone calls, we were set to visit a large, inner-city homeless shelter. But, our contact person at the shelter made it clear that in addition to a tour, the students and I were expected to volunteer for a couple of hours. No problem, according to the students. They were up for the experience.

Or, so it seemed. The day we arrived at the shelter we were ushered to their large industrial kitchen and instructed to put on aprons. Our contact person said we would be assisting with food preparation for the shelter's community wide Thanksgiving dinner, which would take a couple of hours. After that, she said she would take us on a tour.

As we were washing up and putting on aprons, a large smiling man with a knife walked in the kitchen and said, "Hi, I'm Carlos, an ex-crack-cocaine addict. I'm living here in the shelter and working the program. Today, I'm going to show you how to de-bone cooked turkeys for our dinner. Here are your stations and utensils."

He quickly worked around the room, assembling the students into small groups at tables as he demonstrated how to de-bone the turkeys. Many of the students just stood there as if not sure what to do first. But, at least one student in each group took the lead and got the others involved in de-boning and sorting the turkey meat into large aluminum pans for the upcoming dinner.

As we all worked, Carlos shared his story of living on the streets, dealing drugs and ultimately hitting bottom, which landed him in the shelter. It was not a pretty story, yet, one that certainly engaged the students. They started asking questions of Carlos, which propelled him to share even more. As we all worked and listened, I could see groups coming together in ways I had not expected.

After we finished de-boning turkeys, we embarked on a tour of the shelter. The six-story building was laid out much like a college dormitory: small bedrooms, community bathrooms, centralized community rooms, and industrial linoleum. There was a nursery and playroom for small children, but most of the parents and other residents were either working at the shelter or somewhere else, as that was a stipulation of staying at the shelter. The program was explained to us as we finished the tour: to stay at the shelter, residents had to stay "clean" (no drugs, alcohol, etc.), work or look for work, and attend religious classes at the shelter.

As we left that day, students hurried off to get to their next class or work. As much as I wanted immediate feedback from them, I knew I'd have to wait a week, when they returned to class with their reflection papers about the field trip.

During the next class discussion, students shared their impressions, including how surprised they were that the shelter was so clean and organized.

One student commented, "I expected to see a lot of dirty, lazy, drunk people laying around."

Another said, "I nearly fainted when Carlos said we had to cut the meat off the turkeys! I'm a vegetarian and I've never even touched meat before then!"

The student from China said, "Americans are so lucky to have help for homeless people. In our country there is no place to go."

A young male student reflected that "The visit to the shelter hit me like a brick . . . I never realized how lucky I am to have a great family and not want for anything . . . I will never look at life the same again or take things for granted."

Later that day after classes and meetings, I was home with my briefcase full of reflection papers. I brewed some hot tea and settled in to read and grade the papers at my dining room table. I didn't know what to expect. I started reading. It was worth the wait.

For the most part, the papers started off with comments similar to what I heard in class earlier that day. But, as I read further, I was struck by the depth of the connections students made between course concepts like diversity, gender, and nonverbal communication and what they observed and experienced at the shelter. What they saw, and what they did, made the course concepts relevant and real to them. But, more than even that, a sort of serendipity occurred that I had not anticipated: students shattered some of their own stereotypical thinking and wrote about that as well in the papers. Learning, and change, happened.

What I, as a teacher, learned from my students that semester resonates in my teaching practice even now, reminding me that passionate connections to learning are indeed connections that stick and make a difference.

Reflect and respond. As you reflect on the responses from teachers in this chapter, respond to the following questions from the Subject quadrant of The Engaged Teaching and Learning Model:

- How can I make the subject relevant and important to students?
- What are the big issues and questions of the discipline?
- How do professionals in the discipline think?

Engaged Teaching Strategy 5a: Professional Panel

Directions: Invite professionals in fields related to course content to class (three or four is a good size) to talk about what they do and how they apply what they learned in college in their jobs. Help students generate questions to ask the panelists and hold students responsible for asking the questions. At the end of the panel discussion, ask students to give panelists specific feedback about what they learned from the discussion. Inform students ahead of time that they will be expected to do this at the end of the panel discussion so they will take notes.

Expanded Engaged Teaching Strategy 5b: Alumni/Former Student Panel

Directions: Invite former students or alumni (a total of four or five is good) working in fields related to course content to class to talk about what they do and how they apply what they learned in college in their current studies or career fields. Form groups of students and assign each group one of the following tasks: generating questions for the panelists about how to succeed in the course and about careers; facilitating the panel discussion in class; summarizing the panel discussion; and writing follow-up thank you letters to the guest panelists. Expand this strategy by developing an informational interview assignment with former students, a professional, or alumni matched to student career goals. Students write papers based on what they learned about career goals and how to succeed in the course from the interviewees and share their results in class.

Chapter Six

Engaging Students in Active Learning

Tell me and I'll forget; show me and I may remember; involve me and I'll understand.

– Chinese Proverb

Author Narrative: A Teacher as Student

It was a graduate class. I was not naïve; I was familiar with the power structure, the politics, and the culture of higher education, and that is why I was frustrated. Most of all, I expected professionalism in the form of promptness and feedback from the professor.

Our grade was earned on just three essay tests that we took throughout the semester. The problem was that the professor didn't get our tests graded and back to us before the next test rolled around. That was especially crucial to most of the students like me because we needed feedback, not only on how well we did, but also to help us know how to better prepare for the next test. But, it never happened in a timely manner. We eventually got the tests back about two weeks after we'd taken the second test, which gave us a little feedback before the third and final test.

To his credit, the professor was highly likable and friendly. He was always smiling, affable, and delivered fairly interesting lectures. Yet, besides the lack of feedback, he did appear unorganized when he arrived for class.

And, he was always late. We'd all be sitting there in our standard college desks lined up against the walls of the classroom. Waiting. Not saying much, as it was an evening class and I assumed students were tired or just didn't know each other.

When he did arrive, the professor appeared flustered as he shuffled through papers and books at the front of the room. He'd make a little small talk, which was pleasant, but unrelated to the subject. He never stopped smiling. Still, I'd sit there wondering if our tests were in those piles of papers and if we were going to get them back. But, given the implicit student-teacher power hierarchy, it was rare that a student ever asked if he had our graded papers in those piles. I think we all just hoped he had.

Another thing that really bothered me was that he never knew our names. Not once during the entire semester did he address any of us by name. It appeared to me he didn't care or attempt to know our names. Perhaps it wasn't important to him, or he had trouble remembering names. At any rate, he never used our names or seemed interested in learning them — all semester.

The class was made up primarily of young graduate students, and I'm pretty sure I was the only student past the age of 30. I think I was the only college teacher in the class. That was why I minded those things so. I could not imagine taking that much time to get papers graded and back to my students. And, I always learned my students' names as soon as possible, and used their names. Yet, even if I wasn't a teacher, I still minded his lack of attempts at familiarity with students. When a teacher knows your name and uses it, it makes you want to contribute, to do well, and it helps make some students feel like the teacher really cares and values them.

Actually, this unsatisfactory semester as a graduate student was important to me. I took that experience with me to every class I taught from then on. And, I reminded myself how important it is to give students timely feedback, to learn their names, and to show up for class on time.

Reflect and respond. Consider these questions about your teaching practice:

- What are the two or three things that would improve student learning in your classroom, if you did them more often?
- What do you consider your best practice or strategy as a teacher?

- What is your best advice for creating a positive classroom environment?

Ways Teachers Engage Students in Deep Learning

Research generally shows that the amount of retention corresponds to the degree to which a student is dynamically participating in the learning activity.
— Elizabeth Barkley

What do exemplary teachers do when they teach to engage students in deep and significant learning? Setting the stage for engagement with a positive tone from the teacher creates the right conditions, according to Roueche:

I make sure that each and every student feels welcome. Know names, get them actively involved and engaged in the very first class, and keep them positively motivated. Negativity has no place in teaching . . . Teachers who cannot keep students

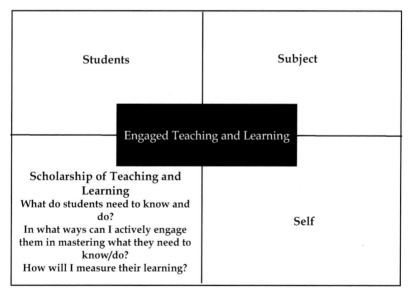

Figure 4. The Engaged Teaching and Learning Model with emphasis on the Scholarship of Teaching and Learning quadrant and key questions teachers need to ask themselves to help engage students in learning.

involved and excited for several hours in the classroom should not be there. (personal communication November 4, 2004)

In the Engaged Teacher Study Survey, the two questions of "What do you do to create a positive learning environment?" and "What do you know and understand as a teacher and professional in your field that helps you engage students in learning?" generated rich descriptions of specific things good teachers do to create positive, charged, and reflective learning environments.

As you read this chapter, think about two things: what you do *before* you teach, and what things you do that you *know* help students learn. Compare your responses with what exemplary teachers in The Engaged Teacher Project say about engaged teaching and learning. In addition, compare what you do with both the anecdotal examples and the expanded research sprinkled throughout this chapter. Take note of the ways that both the teachers' practices and the research specifically relate to the Scholarship of Teaching and Learning component of The Engaged Teaching and Learning Model.

The questions in the model address what engaged teachers know and do to help students learn.

Ways Teachers Build Credibility

Before you can engage students in learning, they need to believe you are credible. Students define credibility differently than do teachers. While teachers equate credibility with expertise in one's field, students equate it with whether you have something valuable that will benefit them considerably, whether you show respect for them and interest in their learning, and whether you follow the policies stated in your syllabus (Bain, 2004; Brookfield, 2006; Huston, 2009).

Specific practices of the teachers in this study illustrate how they establish their credibility in the eyes of students. These responses detail how teachers who responded build credibility with students:

- My first priority is to be well prepared, with back-up material for technology failures. My second is to fully engage my students. I mix lecture with active learning activities, internet and occasionally music. I am an "active" lecturer, meaning

I don't stand at a podium or the front of the room unless it serves a purpose. I prefer to walk among my students making direct eye contact and drawing students into the material. The first thing I remind student of is: THERE IS NO SUCH THING AS A STUPID/DUMB QUESTION and that we are learning as a group. I find that this keeps students relaxed, yet alert, and even helps the shyest student to actively participate in discussion. I use visual props whenever I can and role-play to bring theory out of the heavens and down to earth so students can see how to apply it. I push the "why" behind every decision made; I tell my students if they understand the rationale behind what they are doing/deciding, then they truly understand the theory.

- I plan carefully, reassess all the time what's happening in the classroom . . . I'm flexible when I see a change of some sort will help (slow down, speed up, add/eliminate something, etc.). I get their papers back to them as soon as possible. That's very important—quick feedback. Also, clarity—students are happier in general when they know what's expected of them, and that's the teacher's job. Humor helps enormously . . . no teacher should take herself too seriously, and I don't. I'm not afraid to laugh at myself or something funny that happens in the class; at the same time, I NEVER make fun of a student.

Shared expectations and goals help build teacher credibility. For many teachers, sharing expectations and goals with students helps build credibility. Engaged teachers make clear connections between expectations, goals, and what students do, in turn increasing student buy-in because students then understand the *why* and not just the *what.*

Personally, I try to be clear about expectations on the first day of class by using an active exercise that builds student expectations into the class, which I introduce through action, not announcement. After briefly referring to the course expectation section in the syllabus, I ask students to write three or four expectations they have for the course, fellow students, and the instructor. Then, I group them to describe and discuss their expectations, best college learning experiences, and what they believe should be behavioral and ethical guidelines for the class. We then discuss their responses and how both students and teacher contribute to a successful learning experience in the class, culminating in the creation of course guidelines. See Appendix D for a sample Code of Ethical Classroom Conduct.

After reviewing the learning outcomes and student goals for the course, I ask students to generate examples of how learning the subject will benefit them. We discuss goals and advantages that may not be so obvious, such as increased self-confidence, career earnings, and credibility. Students then work in groups to share their goals and describe the advantages the study of the subject.

In order to encourage trust and disclosure in class, I am welcoming and gracious to the students so they feel comfortable from day one. I am careful with questions and how I ask them, to help students avoid embarrassment and foster participation. Some questions I use are:

- Tell us what you do.
- What questions do you have about the subject or course or teacher or college?
- What are your strengths as a learner?
- What experience or coursework do you have relating to the subject?
- What are your best strategies for succeeding as a student?

Students pair up and use the questions to interview each other for a few minutes. Then, I give them one minute each to introduce their partners to the rest of the class and to share what they found most interesting. I follow up by searching for unique points in their introductions that help them know each other, remember names, and relate the subject to who they are. When I do this, I'm taking notes like crazy for future class assignments, topics of interest, grouping configurations, and reference.

If participation is weak, I try to energize the students during the first class meeting by forming small groups and having them jot down the questions they have about the class. At the same time, I let students know the kind of focused and frequent participation the course requires. Then, together we discuss the "Top Ten List of Questions Students Have on the First Day of Class." While sharing the list, I ask the groups to see if they can find the answers in the syllabus. Some answers are not there, and we discuss those.

These are the questions I pose in countdown fashion after asking students to jot down their questions:

- How much is the textbook, and is it required?
- Do we have to read it?
- Are exams cumulative?
- What are the policies on attendance and late work?
- Where did my instructor go to college?
- Do we have to do group work?
- Where are the best parking spots on campus?
- Can we bring food and drinks to class?
- Where are the bathrooms?
- Are we getting out early today?

The answers to the above are things students like to know on the first day. This activity is an interactive and engaging way to preview the syllabus as well as to incorporate student feedback and questions into the discussion.

There are several things that work well to help students familiarize themselves with policies and expectations in your syllabus. Introducing the syllabus interactively encourages students to use it. If you require students to bring the syllabus to class, say so. I divide students into groups and give them a sheet of questions to be answered using the syllabus. Groups share answers with the entire class. This helps me diagnose where students need more help or information.

Another first day strategy is to arrive early to reconfigure the seating arrangement in the classroom, if possible, to form a U-shape. I make large name tents for each student, printing their names with a bold tip marker that can be seen from across the room. I tell them I do this when I teach for corporations in the "real" world, just as our classroom is the "real" world. I also ask them to relate to each other regularly and respectfully, by name, thus taking away the embarrassment of failing to remember names during discussions. This helps students (and myself) save face and makes engaging with others in class easier.

Students leave the class after the first day with less anxiety and more information about what to expect the rest of the semester. The students engage with other students and the teacher in activities that relate to the subject and to learning. And, they begin to know their classmates. This helps create a community of learners.

Barriers to student motivation and engagement. Experts report that credibility and authenticity are characteristics students value highly in teachers. Yet, Brookfield (2006) explains how student resistance to thinking and learning can negate the most credible teacher's efforts:

> I know that modeling critical thinking is crucial to helping students learn it, but that students will probably resist critical thinking whatever I do. I know too that resistance to learning is a highly predictable presence in my classrooms and that its very presence does not mean I'm a failure. And I know that I cannot motivate anyone to learn if at a very basic level they don't wish to. All I can do is try to remove whatever organizational, psychological, cultural, interpersonal, or pedagogic barriers are getting in the way of them learning, provide whatever modeling I can, build the best possible case for learning, and then cross my fingers and hope for the best. (p. 14)

Overcoming barriers to student motivation and engagement. How do excellent teachers overcome these obstacles? Teachers in this study shared these ideas:

- Each student comes with their particular goals, insecurities and knowledge and skill set and you meet them where they are and see what you can do together to progress. I believe my students, particularly at a community college, are hardworking, down-to-earth, very deserving of the opportunity to grow and succeed, and full of life experiences that we can only begin to tap in the classroom. I like to look for students' strengths and use them as models for the principles we are focusing on.
- I try to treat students with respect, sensitivity, compassion, and approach any struggling students by reaching out to them and asking what I can do to help . . . I also expect students to make their education a priority, even though many students have obstacles and roadblocks that get in the way. I sincerely invite students to privately communicate these to me immediately, so we can work through their difficult problems.

- While acknowledging each student as an individual, and while seeking ways to encourage, I offer specific advice on how he or she might stretch and grow. Over the years I've learned to be more direct and precise about this, to look a student in the eye and say, 'Right here is something strong or promising' or 'this is necessary' or 'this won't do.' If my directness confuses a student, I assure them I am their advocate, am on their side, and offer the advice out of kindness.
- I periodically do spot-check assignments to see if students understand materials. I also mix lecture with discussion and experiential learning. I try to challenge them to think critically about the material. I try to tap into various learning styles and try to reach all the styles with the material. I also ask students to be responsible for units or reading for the class — they also learn by being responsible and engaging in others.
- Reward success—provide frequent feedback, establish clear goals and expectations, talk to students one on one, discover individual interests, build on those things.

Learning more about how students learn. There are many helpful tools that can easily be introduced in nearly any class you teach. Brookfield's Critical Incident Questionnaire (2006) is a quick, revealing and anonymous way to discover the effects your teaching actions are having on student learning and classroom climate. Report the results back to students quickly to build trust and credibility. Another useful tool to help reveal the knowledge students bring into the class is the Background Knowledge Probe. (Angelo & Cross, 1993). It is not a measure of performance, nor is it graded. Students complete it anonymously and you use it as an assessment tool to identify what you'll need to explain in more detail. Many teachers in this study said they use classroom research and assessment tools, learning inventories, and feedback measures, particularly those developed by Angelo and Cross (1993). Recommended literature on teaching and learning in Appendix A will help you as you develop your own teaching practice.

Ways to Engage Students with the Subject

One of the reasons many students don't engage in learning is that they don't see the connections between the subject and how it will benefit them. Exemplary teachers help close that gap by giving students the WIIFM — "What's In It For Me" — to illustrate relevance. Here are some of the ways teachers responding to the survey said help to bring the learning process to life for students:

- I supplement key principles of my subject with appropriate contemporary media or pop culture into instruction. I find this increases appeal to today's students and engages them in critical thinking.

- I bring in interesting guest speakers and former students close to the ages of my students to talk about success in their field, how they work, how they think, why they love what they do, and how to network.

- I require all my students to do fieldwork, which helps them fairly quickly realize if they are cut out for the profession. Also, it engages the student in ways I could never do in class alone and gives such rich subject matter for class discussion.

- I really try to get to know my students: what they are proud of, what their goals are, where they work, what they like or don't like, how they learn best, what they consider their strengths and weaknesses, etc. I make adjustments in how I teach constantly based on how I can best connect to each student, their needs, their learning strengths and weaknesses, etc. I have them complete learning style inventories and develop goals they have for the course and do periodic checks. I let them choose service projects from options they create. I make them responsible for teaching each other and sharing their work. I ask them questions and listen, really listen, because that builds relationships and trust! Students <u>do</u> something related to the subject at hand.

- One technique that I like to use is to have students take a theory or concept that is addressed in the current chapters and write a three-paragraph essay on it. The first paragraph should explain or define the concept. The second paragraph should provide an original example of the concept from the real world. This could be a personal experience, a cartoon, an example from the newspaper, song lyrics, or an example from a movie. The third paragraph should describe how this illustration exemplifies the concept or theory selected. This essay is then shared in small groups during the class and included for points on their test. My goal is to model this technique as a way of personalizing the material and facilitating storage and retrieval of information. Students come up with great illustrations and insights using this technique.

A retired professor turned storyteller reflected on his use of stories in the classroom and shared, "I find, that when I tell a story appropriate to the lesson, receptive listening and retention increases. I also attempt to take the content of the lesson and relate it as much as possible to the daily lives of the students."

Learner-centered approaches to teaching. Weimer's (2002) focus on learner-centered teaching embraces active learning principles in an attempt to reach poorly prepared students who resist deep learning. Teachers report many unprepared students prefer shallowness because it requires less work. Nonetheless, increasing the focus on what and how students are learning has the effect of engaging students in the course and its content.

There are many types of learner-centered approaches: increasing decisions students can make, providing a variety of assignments, and applying content through active learning strategies such as writing-to-learn activities, service-learning, and cooperative learning.

Here are some of the ways teachers in this study described their approaches to active, learner-centered teaching:

- I know that students must become engaged in the process for good learning to take place. They must find the material relevant, i.e. see how it connects to their lives. I am a big proponent of . . . active learning via hands-on-labs and demonstrations, collaborative learning, collective problem solving and visual learning using illustrations, role playing, Power Point or online animations.
- I started using problem-based learning in my classroom several years ago and then moved on to service-learning in most of my courses because it gets students involved in applied

learning that brings the subject to life for them, especially when the reflection assignment is well developed.

- The questions I ask myself before I teach are:
  - Is there an active way to present the material to get the students moving, touching, practicing, rather than sitting?
  - Is there a way to bring the students' experiences into the classroom to make the information more meaningful?
  - Does this information assist the students in becoming a better professional? If so, use it. If not, ditch it.
  - Does the way I am presenting the information cause the student to be passive? If so, how can I make them active and solve problems?
  - Did the students learn the information well enough to teach it to others? Then I have them teach it to others—a spouse, friend, child, parent, etc.
  - Did the student learn the information well enough to generalize it to a new situation or case study?
  - Did the student learn anything from me? Assess it.
  - Do I mentor the students in behavior, excitement, respect, and problem solving skills?

Other learner-centered approaches teachers cited included giving students a choice of assignments, allowing groups to generate topics for papers and presentations, and having students teach each other concepts from the textbook not covered in class. The question teachers need to continually ask when using a learner-center approach is "How are my students thinking, applying and using the content?"

Weimer (2002) comments on active learning techniques in learner-centered environments:

> Active learning is not a set of tricks to use with basically bored students. It is a powerful tool with well-established results. Those results, however, accrue only when active learning strategies involve content. Whatever it is the students are doing should involve legitimate, bona-fide course content. (pp. 52-53)

Active learning pedagogies. Learning communities, collaborative learning, problem-based learning, and service learning

---

are pedagogies that actively engage students. Palmer (1998) describes applying "subject-centered classrooms" and new learning through the use of service-learning programs:

> . . .consider the service-learning programs that are flourishing on more and more campuses these days, programs that place students in community activities related to the field they are studying. In a large political science class at a state university, three-fourths of the students were assigned a normal syllabus while the remainder were assigned all of that plus a field placement. One might think that the latter students would suffer academically; after all, they had to spend extra time and energy on field assignments and might even have resented that fact. But those students did *better* academically and became more personally and substantively engaged with the course because the great things they met by being involved with the community made their bookwork more real. (p. 118)

My own experience with service-learning evolved over the years, beginning with collaborative, problem-based, learning approaches in my classes. I developed case studies based on real situations I experienced as a trainer for industry, health care, and law enforcement. I wanted students to develop a stronger sense of how professionals in the field think. I took students into the community to experience hands-on learning.

In my introductory speech course, I developed a School Storytellers service project. Students perform stories in elementary classrooms as volunteers. The assignment comes in the midpoint of the semester. Skills students need to improve at this point are vocal variety, gestures, facial expressions, and movement. The learning objectives of this assignment include audience analysis, vocal and visual delivery skills, group problem-solving, and civic engagement.

When I first introduce this assignment, students ask the following questions: "Do we have to drive to a school to do it? Won't the kids be bored? How are we graded?"

When we get through some of the initial questions, students feel more comfortable. I map out where the school is located and discuss carpooling logistics. I bring in guest speakers (former students and professional storytellers) to help the students master effective storytelling skills.

As an assessment before the assignment, students respond in writing to the following:
- What are your fears, hopes, and expectations for the School Storytellers assignment?
- What strengths as a speaker or group member do you bring to this assignment?
- What specific areas do you need to work on to be an effective School Storyteller?

Preparation includes interactive drills giving students opportunities to improve all the required aspects of the assignment: delivery skills, voices, gestures and body movements. Students work in assigned groups to rehearse story selections recommended by the elementary teachers, matched to the reading and literacy levels of their students.

This pivotal assignment helps strengthen the students' delivery skills, confidence, and team-building abilities. They return from this assignment as stronger speakers and actually look forward to the final few speeches in class. After the assignment, students complete a feedback and assessment summary geared to assess their learning and experience. The assessment is included in Appendix E.

In addition to improved speaking skills, this service-learning experience helps students develop sensitivity with diverse audiences and expands their awareness of community needs. They return to the college classroom energized and motivated to improve, armed with increased competency in speaking, greater confidence in their ability to adapt to audiences, and a heightened awareness and interest in community service. Many students continue to volunteer after completing this assignment.

Technology and student learning. Teaching and learning technologies are exploding on campuses today. The challenge for many instructors has been integrating online teaching or a course management system into their practices. Although most of the insights about engaged teaching and learning can be applied to both face-to-face classroom teaching and online teaching, the context for learning can pose more challenges when teaching a course online. Here is one teacher's reluctant technology journey:

Teacher Snapshot: From Reluctant to Renewed

I was skeptical when I began to convert a class to an online format necessitated by student demand and institutional initiatives. For a visual person like myself, I struggle with the lack of visual and vocal cues and nuances when communicating with students asynchronously in my online courses. I've done a few things to compensate that have helped me and my students develop more of an engaging online learning experience:

- I send out emails one to three times a week to students and label them "Friendly Reminders/Updates for (course name)" in the subject line.
- I use a conversational tone in my emails and feedback to students. I use their names and write as if I were speaking to them in person.
- I build community among students in weekly discussion boards where interaction is required in the form of students commenting back to each other's comments to my questions and prompts.
- I give students individual comments and feedback on all the work they submit.
- I highly recommend students attend the on-campus orientation I conduct before the class begins; during this meeting and in my course syllabus I make the rigor and demands of the course explicit so students know exactly what to expect—a learning experience that requires strong time management, motivation, writing skills, and commitment. I also encourage them to come meet me on campus and make myself available at their convenience.
- I give students my home phone number in case of an emergency.

Brookfield's (2006) suggestions are extremely helpful in shaping online courses to increase student awareness of their own learning. He suggests taking online courses from colleagues and increasing communication with online students. He remarks, "The number one complaint for online learners is the low level of instructor responsiveness. Students clearly need to hear from us on a regular basis" (p. 199).

Chapter Summary

Most of the engaged teaching practices reported by teachers in this study reinforce what research has discovered about effective instruction. Frequent student-faculty connections and contact are important factors in student motivation and involvement. Knowledge about learning and about one's students helps instructors engage students' desire to know and learn. Learner-centered teaching climates produce motivated and responsible learners. Engaged teachers know as much about the learning process as they do about their subject matter.

Author Narrative: The Phone Call

It was a sunny late October afternoon, with rust-colored leaves whirling and the chill of fall in the air. I was raking in the yard when I missed a phone call. I saw the message light blinking when I walked into the house later that afternoon.

I pushed the voicemail button and heard, "Hello, Nancy, this is Seth."

"Wow," I thought, "my former student Seth! I haven't heard from him in ages!" I continued to listen as he said the following:

> I have the unusual opportunity to have some free time driving home from a talk I just gave this morning in Iowa. I was listening to a CD series on public speaking and I remember the opportunities you gave us in our public speaking class... I have such great memories of such great teaching on your part, and I wanted to thank you for that introduction. I'm now moving full-time into speaking, seminars, educational publications, books, and some others things.
>
> I wanted to thank you for all those years of teaching and the impact you've made in my life and probably in all those lives of other people. Well, I want you to know that I'm moving full time into public speaking and really living my dreams... so, thank you, thank you, thank you. I hope you are well. Bye for now.

After I listened to Seth's message, I took a few minutes to take stock of what he had said. It's rare to receive that kind of feedback from a former student.

The Seth I met years ago as a student had all the raw material for greatness: intellect, curiosity, creativity, charisma and drive. I felt like I'd won the student lotto to have him in my class and my learning community. In his own words, years after he graduated, here is his account:

I was a high school drop out. . . I started community college at 19. . . Frankly, I was in a period of recovery. . . It was a critical time. . . There are people that you meet when you are working your way towards a dream. They take your hand and help you out of the past. Sometimes that person is a teacher. Some professors are outrageously optimistic but lack rigor. In other situations, the professor demonstrates rigor and instills trust, but opts to put in only the minimum effort. Then there are those professors that instill confidence in their students, establish rigorous standards and create change in their environment. That is what I had with two of my community college teachers. Now I am a professional speaker and best-selling author, and winning awards as a speaker. How did my teachers influence this? Here's how:

They impelled me toward a more confident version of myself. . . One of my teachers invited me to work on a documentary on the creative process, which was paid for by a grant. . . allowing me to dig into material I loved and develop practical material for portfolio work. As a result of one-on-one mentoring, I have had the confidence to go on and create books, plays and CDs of original music.

They expected the best from me in [their] class. . . They knew when I had given 100% or when I had done enough to get by. They make the campus a better place. . . with tangible contributions: Books, film, speaker series, speaking sincerely, expressing genuine interest, taking time with students. I was one of those students. It was 11 years ago that I graduated with an Associate's Degree from a community college. . . I keep in touch with two of my professors there. I tell them, "You impacted my life. Thank you for the impeccable quality you bring to your work. You are an unsung hero. Don't ever wonder if your work makes a difference. You are extraordinary."

I believe that there are millions more students out there whose lives have been influenced by a teacher in a similar way. As great as that kind of feedback is, whether we get it or not, we continue our teaching practice with the belief that we are changing lives. That may even be the reason we do what we do each day. We didn't become teachers because we wanted to be rich or famous. I believe that many, like me, became teachers because we care about students and we want to make a difference in the world. Idealistic? Maybe. But, great teachers can help students transcend barriers and succeed.

Reflect and respond. Reflect on the following questions related to the Scholarship of Teaching and Learning quadrant from The Engaged Teaching and Learning Model:

- What do students need to know and do?
- In what ways can I actively engage them in mastering what they need to know/do?
- How will I measure their learning?

Engaged Teaching Strategy 6a: Group Concept Role Plays/Skits

Directions: Form groups of three or four students and ask them to pool what they know about a key course concept from the readings (assign a different concept to each group). Based on their knowledge, they are to create and perform a two-minute skit or role-play to "teach" the concept to the rest of the class. Debrief with discussion of how students illustrated the concepts.

Expanded Engaged Teaching Strategy 6b: Online Group Power Point Lessons

Directions: This group exercise can be executed in an online course or in a face-to-face course using a course management system where students communicate and work together electronically outside of class. Form groups of four to five students and create a group drop box online giving only the group members access. Create a graded assignment with a rubric requiring the groups to create a Power Point slide presentation to "teach" the rest of the class about a key course concept (assign concepts or give choice to groups). Post the Power Point presentations on the course site for all students to view; provide feedback to the groups privately. Be specific about time frames for this project and require periodic updates to monitor student participation and progress. Allow students to post feedback to the group presentations.

Chapter Seven

Exploring Teaching Insights

We develop a scholarship of teaching when our work as teachers becomes public, peer-reviewed and critiqued, and exchanged with other members of our professional communities so they, in turn, can build on our work.
— Lee Shulman

Teachers need to be actively learning from their teaching.
— Elizabeth Barkley

Author Narrative: Reality Intrudes

It started unlike most other mornings in Mrs. Berg's math class. She was late, which was unusual. All the students waiting for her in the classroom heard the rapid clomp-clomp-clomp of her short heels on the well-worn hardwood hallway floor as she neared our door. She was always in the classroom before we arrived; this morning she was five minutes late. She wasn't one of those teachers who habitually walked in late smelling like the sour smoke of the teachers' lounge. She always looked and smelled good. And, she always entered the room with a smile and a warm "Good morning, class."

Not that morning. She just walked in. We knew by the look in her eyes that something was wrong. "Was she disappointed with our work? Did someone die?" We all wondered what had happened. We had no idea, but knew that something was wrong.

Mrs. Berg was silent. Her shoulders were slumped and her face was drawn. We'd never seen that look before. We waited. She didn't say anything for what seemed like a very long time. Then she looked at us. Each of us. She scanned the room, slowly absorbing us with her eyes as if it were the first time she really saw us. Mrs. Berg's slow, steady gaze commanded silence. No one spoke. Not a word. Not one pencil dropped. Not one student coughed. The only sounds were the squeaky spots in the floor as Mrs. Berg slowly paced back and forth behind her desk. A sweet early springtime breeze blew in the gigantic windows, reminding us we could feel. We waited. We waited for Mrs. Berg to begin, and she did.

"What kind of a world are we living in when four students are gunned down by the National Guard on a college campus? What kind of a world are we living in when parents send their children away to college and they are shot to death? What kind of a world are we living in?"

Her questions stunned us and we sat in silence, waiting for her to explain. She did explain. She told us about the Kent State University shootings at an anti-Vietnam war protest on the campus. She told us the story she had heard on the news that morning in the teachers' lounge. As she told us, we could hear her heart breaking.

I don't remember doing math that morning at all. But, I do remember that my world changed. The world all of us were living in changed forever.

Reflect and respond. Consider the questions below as you explore your insights:

- What significant events affected you as a student? How did they influence you?
- In what class did you learn the most? What was it about you or the teacher at the time that led to your learning?
- Do you do anything that helps you re-experience being a student? What have you learned from that process that you can bring to the classroom?

How We Teach Is Who We Are

> We are what we repeatedly do. Excellence, therefore, is not an
> act, but a habit.
>> —Aristotle

Sometimes it takes a figurative whack on the side of the head to awaken us to the lessons we miss because we're too busy or just not listening. Perhaps it's a scathing student evaluation that surprises us. It could be a student's apathetic attitude that unnerves us, despite our best efforts in class. It could be teaching a course online for the first time, or even using a new course management system. We might react with doubts about remaining a teacher, wondering if we should in fact take up another career.

During such times, we often look outside of ourselves for answers. Yet, it is precisely these times of self-doubt when it helps to reconnect to who we are and why we became teachers. A small, inner voice emanating from our heart asks: "Who am I as a teacher? What informs my teaching practices? Do I trust what I know?" It is time to reflect and listen.

To grow and improve as teachers, we need to take time to reflect on those questions, as they shape the way we teach. We need to listen to our inner voices as we examine what we need to do, what works and what doesn't. We need to remember, too, that what we don't say or do may be as important as what we do say or do.

As described by a student, here is one teacher's first day approach:

Student Snapshot: First Day

Was he shy? Was his silence intentional? Was this one of those weird tests some instructors gave on the first day of class to analyze our personalities? It was uncomfortable for a few minutes, but then as soon as he started talking—quietly and tentatively—he drew us in to listen in a way that was much deeper and more intimate than I'd ever experienced before. He asked us to rearrange the desk chairs in a circle. Since there were only 15 of us in the class that brought us in quite close to each other, closer than I was used to with a room full of strangers. But, it was okay because of the gentle way he asked us to do it: "Would you all mind if we rearranged the chairs to form a circle? Could you help me with that, please?" And, we did. Then, silence again. He looked at us, slowly meeting our gazes, as a small smile crept across his face. His eyes were smiling, too. That was what made it so real. It was not a phony "hello, first day of class" smile like some teachers pasted across their faces when they walked in the room and said "hello" without looking at you. It was a real smile. With it, I believe we were all much more relaxed and at ease on this first day of Personal Writing, an advanced writing class at the college.

Next, he said we were going to do a version of the "Name Game" to get to know a bit about each other. A slight groan resonated from several students, but he was unwavering as he began with the instructions: "Let's go around the circle and introduce ourselves, sharing something about yourself that you'd like the rest of the class to know and remember. I'll begin if you like." So, he did. He introduced himself as if he were one of us, asking us to call him by his first name, Skip. He told us he liked to jog in his spare time, and that would help us remember his name.

We all followed in similar fashion, trying to think of something clever or logical or memorable to say. Skip commented between the introductions, relating to what students said or the likenesses among students in the class. "That's an interesting name," or "You must have a long drive to college," or "Your job might provide some powerful ideas to write about." With each comment he made to our introductions, he shared a bit of information about himself. By the end, we knew a little about each other, and our teacher, and the tension in the classroom dissipated as we all felt a tad connected to each other. The slow pace and gentle self-disclosure orchestrated by the teacher was comforting, relaxing, and inviting. It made me eager to learn.

Your first days of classes may look nothing like this, and that's okay. You need not imitate someone else's teaching practice. Rather, I hope this helps you take the time to analyze what others do and glean insights that you can bring to your own teaching practice.

Reflect and respond. As you discover and analyze what other teachers do, consider these two questions about what you do and how effective it is.

- On the first day of class, why do you do what you do, if anything, to reveal who you are or what your teaching philosophy is to your students?

- What guides the way you teach your class, the order of things, the way you communicate expectations to students, and the type and frequency of feedback you give students?

A special kind of courage is required to engage in honest self-analysis as an ongoing practice apart from evaluation and promotion times. Reflective practice implores us to analyze what we do by sharing our practices with others and adjusting them to become a better teacher. Such honest appraisals help avoid the "trap of teaching behind closed doors" that closes us off from feedback and can lead to professional isolation.

In this chapter, the insights and reflective practices emerging from the exemplary teachers participating in The Engaged Teacher Survey are the focus. As you read, think about your own reflections and insights and how they guide your teaching.

The Self component of The Engaged Teaching and Learning Model addresses the kinds of knowledge and self-awareness we gain through meaningful reflection. It contains feedback from others, and requires continual assessment of our effectiveness in the classroom.

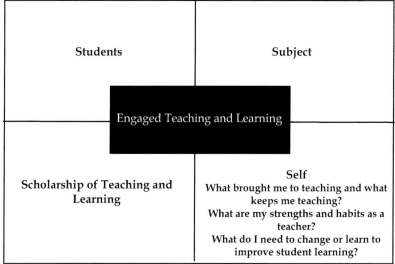

Figure 5. The Engaged Teaching and Learning Model with emphasis on the Self quadrant and key questions teachers need to ask themselves to raise knowledge and self-awareness regarding their teaching effectiveness.

How Reflection Drives the Practices of Engaged Teachers

Here are examples of how teachers interpret nonverbal behavior in the classroom, react on the spot, reflect on the nonverbal feedback, and adjust accordingly to keep students engaged:

- Ah, the eyes have it. After teaching for over 25 years it is easy for me to look into the eyes of the crowd and know whether they are engaged or disengaged. If I sense they are not engaged I change gears. If I'm lecturing I continuously ask questions and break for small collaborative activities followed by reporting back to the class.
- I gauge the climate of the classroom. I walk around the room constantly. I tell them often how much I love my job. I look at every student throughout the class. I read the facial expressions of the students and change my behavior accordingly. I can tell when things are clicking with the students, I can tell when things are not clicking and I change according. I leave many days thinking I am a terrible teacher because I didn't fully engage the class. I work harder the next day.

The teachers in the study talked about the importance of observing and knowing students in order to engage them intellectually, motivate them, and relate to them personally. The more they knew about students, the better they could engage them in meaningful and relevant ways. Engaged teachers foster authentic and reciprocal relationships that create shared responsibility for learning. They focus on students' strengths and weaknesses, how to make the subject relevant, and how to best motivate students, as illustrated in the next Student Snapshot.

Student Snapshot: A Teacher's Encouragement Made the Difference

I've had few very good teachers. My Psychology teacher was the best teacher I've ever had. He took the time to patiently explain theories that I didn't understand, to read rough drafts I'd written to help me find my mistakes, as well as to give me advice on what I needed to add or omit. He was very kind and very inspiring. If I ever needed encouragement, he would gladly give it. He always told me to NEVER settle for simply passing. I stayed after class one day to ask a question about my study journal when my grades became a subject of conversation between us. After learning that I was pretty much a straight A student, my teacher asked why I wasn't getting all A's in HIS class?

'I'm good with getting a C in this class,' I said with a shrug. Of course I wanted an A, but Psychology was a tough subject for a first semester of college. I didn't have faith in myself to get an A. I couldn't grasp a lot of the material.

My teacher gave me a doubtful look and replied, 'Shoot for an A! Why settle for less? It's always better to try your hardest than to coast. If you coast, you might fail. If you give it your all, you will always pass. I have faith in you.'

Those words are still with me, and they always will be. Whether he knows it or not, his words have impacted me strongly. I realized that his encouragement doesn't just apply to school. It applies to life. If you coast in life, you might fail. If you try your hardest, you will more than likely succeed. Of course failure occurs in every part of life, sometimes despite how much we try. But isn't it better to try and fail than to not try at all? I think so! At the end of my first semester, I passed Psychology (and the other two classes I was taking at the time) with an A . . . and it was the most rewarding A I'd ever received!

Insights from the Engaged Teacher Survey

Insights about self: What engaged teachers understand

- I constantly ask myself "why," as it relates to everything... the grade I give, the rubric I put together, the assignment I give, etc. Too, I constantly reflect on how my practices and philosophies compare to what I "know" about other faculty, and I discuss with other faculty these assumptions (but most faculty feel threatened by and are hostile to such discussions).
- I listen, listen, listen. I try to understand literally what students say to me as well as the subtext of it, the body language of it, to really hear them... I speak frankly to them, one on one and in the whole group (although not embarrassing anyone in front of the whole group)... But a teacher has to be able to say, 'What you have done so far isn't good enough. If you

keep doing this, you will fail this class.' The first few years I taught, I really had a hard time doing that. I would be too oblique about it. Now, I just tell it to them straight . . . I also offer whatever help is appropriate . . . And I say it in a neutral tone, no judgment attached.

- I disclose appropriately to my students to help them connect to and trust me. I want them to know that even I, the teacher/ expert, was once a scared, insecure student. I share stories of how I failed, and what I did to pick myself up and get back on track. I tell them I am a first generation college student. I help them assess their learning strengths and constantly gather classroom feedback to learn what helps them learn and what I could do to be more effective.
- I tune in to what troubles me: students that don't try, circumstances I can't change or control, other pressing demands in my own life. I try to sort through those and come up with ways to keep my sanity as a teacher. Things that help me include: enforcing course policies, color coding my course packs, physical exercise, and sharing ups and downs with colleagues.
- When I teach, I would liken it to jazz. A good jazz musician will prepare for a concert but will take advantage of the moment, the synergy, the players there on that day. And, any of us might really play a bad note and you just go on. Humor helps. There is a "flow" in the classroom when things are going right and humming along. And sometimes there is not, and that's when you sing the blues a little internally, and figure out a way to push past it.

Insights about subject: What engaged teachers know
- I come to class with the perspective of having just been out in the field — understanding where they are coming from. Most of my students are currently working in the field so they need to know that I understand what it's like. I spend a lot of time going out into the field, volunteering... getting to know what it's like in the field today so we can talk about that. I try to approach any theory or textbook learning by applying it directly to their required fieldwork experiences.

- Good teachers have knowledge both of disciplinary content and best teaching practices. A good teacher knows the essential questions of his or her discipline and routinely designs course study in the light of those questions.
- A good teacher knows the subject content. That is first and foremost the most important. Process is also important, but you need the content! A "good" teacher also knows the process of teaching. They are passionate and approachable. A "good" teacher is also flexible (i.e. willing to update material, try new technologies, etc.).
- I think students learn best when they see the subject matter as relevant to their personal lives. Students remember things that involve active participation and student engagement. Students also learn best when expectations for performance are clear and the bar is held high. Students learn well with frequent feedback and encouragement. Students also try harder when they think their professor truly cares about them and their success. There are new developments and changes in the research in my field all the time, so I must stay engaged as a professional in the research in my field. I use research-based practices. I explain why I do what I do to students.

Insights about students: How engaged teachers connect to students

- Get to know them [students]—one-on-one discussions are the only way to build a lasting student/teacher relationship. Compliments build confidence and motivate them to reach their full potential. I periodically remind them to kick it up a notch so that they know my expectations are high.
- I really try to get to know my students: what they are proud of, what their goals are, where they work, what they like/don't like, how they learn best, what they consider their strengths and weaknesses, etc. I make adjustments in how I teach constantly based on how I can best connect to each student, their needs, their learning strengths and weaknesses, etc. I have them each develop goals they have for the course and do periodic checks. I let them choose service projects from options they create. I make them responsible for teaching each other and sharing their work. I ask them questions and listen, really listen, because that builds relationships and

trust. And students that trust you as a teacher are bound to invest more and learn more!

- I approach teaching like coaching track and field. I don't expect students to run the mile at the beginning of the semester as fast as they can at the end of the semester when they are in peak performance. We expect everyone to be on the same playing field, which is unrealistic and will never happen. We have to constantly gauge our students and ourselves and ask what works and why, then make adjustments.

Insights about teaching and learning: What engaged teachers do

- There is so much I've used to help students: active learning, problem-based learning, collaborative learning, summative and formative classroom assessment, service-learning, and now brain-based learning.
- I joined a faculty learning community and it helped me analyze the way I teach. It was a cross-disciplinary group that met for one year. The learning community helped me embed three habits: keep current both in my field and in the research on teaching and learning, constantly examine the process of learning in my classroom, and seek feedback from other teaching colleagues.
- When I became I teacher, I knew little about teaching. All of my coursework had been in my subject matter. I was thrown into teaching a full course load and advised to take advantage of professional development opportunities at my college. Who has time for that? Between departmental meetings, college committees, course prep, and office hours, I was doing all I could to stay one lesson ahead of my students. I went to the faculty center library and picked up some books to read over the summer. I try to read at least two books on teaching and learning every summer. It helped me understand a lot about students, how they are different, and how they learn.

The Engaged Teacher Study responses correspond to what Bain (2004) found: Most of the teachers he analyzed have generally woven together their teaching practices and conceptions of human learning from their direct experiences with students. Their teaching practices include some sort of ongoing appraisal to reflect on their progress and make appropriate changes to improve student learning. Bain states that their practices "are remarkably similar to some ideas that have emerged in the research and theoretical literature on cognition, motivation and human development" (p. 25-6).

How Mentors Influence Us

Mentors influence how we teach; for many teachers, a mentor's influence stays with them. How often do you notice yourself saying or doing something your mentor said? Intrator (2002) characterizes the strength of a strong mentor's influence:

> Great teachers who touched us in profound ways when we were students imprint deeply on how we think about our own teaching. The gift of our mentors is that they awaken in us ideas of how we think about our subject matter and a sense of how we can touch the lives of our students. (p. 126)

Teacher Snapshot: My Mentor, Me

I can see how much I modeled my own teaching on my mentor's influence, not trusting my own experience or preparation when I began teaching. I was always asking myself, 'What would my mentor do?'

Like many teachers, I began teaching the way my mentor taught, even down to the way I dressed. When I spoke in class, I tried to sound like my mentor. Many times I felt like an inferior version of my mentor.

Years into my teaching career, while team teaching with my mentor, he turned to me and said, "I don't consider myself your mentor anymore. I consider you my equal."

To me, his statement was permission to be myself, trust myself, and rely on my own insights, training, and experience at this point in my teaching career. As a result, I grew as a teacher. Evidence from my students demonstrated they were more engaged and learning more. I trusted myself more with creative approaches and new pedagogies.

Now, as a "veteran" teacher, I give my students more responsibility for their learning and empower them to learn collaboratively. I trust my instincts, experience, and continue to learn. Now, that voice in the classroom is my own.

Finding Our Voices as Teachers

In finding our voices as teachers, we may go through the process described by Parini (2005):

> Teachers, like writers, also need to invent and cultivate a voice, one that serves their personal needs as well as the material at hand, one that feels authentic. It should also take into account the nature of the students who are being addressed, their background in the subject and their disposition as a class. (p. 58)

O'Banion describes how he authentically uses his voice to help students:

> I know I have to help students connect who they really are (their values, ideas, hopes, needs, experience) with some body of knowledge or skills they need. I bring myself to the table as fully and as authentically as the situation allows and use my whole self to push and prod and cajole the students to do the same. (personal communication, June 14, 2009)

A teacher's reflection illustrates the power of voice and authority in the classroom:

Teacher Snapshot: Reflection Hurts

Once, I showed a short documentary on gender socialization in mass media. Afterwards, I asked the class their thoughts... a female student (who I did not like... she didn't often come to class, but when she did, she sought to "challenge" my authority with what I considered ill-founded and naive opinions) said loudly and with some hostility "That's a lie!"

The class was shocked and quiet. I stood there for a moment... a moment I wish I could take back — and then I told her to leave the room. I was angry, angry that she dared to confront what I thought was "the truth" of the documentary, and angry that she would do so in such a hostile manner. I was angry that she had seemingly dismissed any consideration of the subject [and] that I dismissed her.

I have regretted that moment ever since, and it is a constant reminder to me that I was being a hypocrite... I said then

I wanted students to think about and understand the world, yet I had not provided any room for that... instead what I had really done in my practice that day was exert my authority, my understanding, my way of thinking upon her and others in the classroom by closing off the opportunity for students to negotiate the material.

Ironically, years later when I began an EdD program, I was like the girl in the story above... by this time, I was more engaged with aspects of critical thinking, and had started asking critical thinking of my discipline, and of my teaching. But, in the classroom as a student, I more than once experienced that MY teachers were not open to such a discussion of the subject THEY were teaching... and it made me angry. Who were they to say that my experiences and observations were wrong? Why were we not asking questions about the very nature of knowledge, and more importantly, the pros/cons of research and knowledge?

Every time that I felt like one of MY doctoral professors was cutting me off, and/or dismissing the very legitimate question I raised, I remembered the girl I sent from the room. Since then... every day is a reminder of MY power in establishing a "true" learning experience... versus just providing room for me to talk and assert a "truth" about the world. Every day I think about the ethical implications of the power I have as a teacher, in the classroom, and ultimately, in the world. It is a huge responsibility, and one I take seriously.

Summary

Many of the teachers in The Engaged Teacher Study attributed much of what they know and practice as teachers to experience, intuition, and the influence of mentors, students, and colleagues. Some mentioned exploring teaching pedagogies and learning theory on their own or through professional development. Regardless of the approaches cited, it is clear that teachers are always digging deeper into their subject, how to teach it effectively, and constantly looking for ways to understand how students learn.

Overall, the teachers responding to the survey see themselves as reflective learners, regularly analyzing ways to improve their teaching practice and foster student development. They want to know as much as possible about their subject and how best to teach it. They are reflective about their own journey as both teacher and learner, and they encourage students to be reflective about their own learning. Many described how they use ongoing appraisal of their progress and make appropriate changes. They continue to learn, and they inspire their students to challenge themselves as learners.

Author Narrative: Reality, Again

Fast-forward 33 years later, when I was a teacher at a community college in the Midwest, I experienced another world-changing day in the classroom. It was September 11, 2001. Although I had no idea at the time, the events of that day would come to have a huge influence on the way I teach. That day marked a turning point in my life as a teacher. My students and I embarked on a different kind of journey that changed the way I taught and took learning out of the classroom.

It was a Tuesday morning. I was meeting the 21 students in my 8 to 11 a.m. Interpersonal Communications class for the third time that semester. Right after that class, I had a three-hour Public Speaking class. When I finished up with the first class, I immediately headed for my classroom for the 11 a.m. class because we were going to hear a speaker that day in the large lecture hall at the college.

When we arrived, we learned the guest speaker had been canceled and a live news report from CNN was being projected on the huge screen in the lecture hall. What we saw shocked us all. Images of two jet airplanes plowing into the Twin Towers in New York City were being broadcast over and over again as the commentator tried to make sense of it all. Stunned, we sat down and listened, trying to figure it out ourselves as we absorbed the haunting images. No one spoke.

Just two months earlier, while in Manhattan myself, I had taken the subway to the World Trade Center to buy theater tickets. That recent foray to the city stuck in my mind as I watched the newscast. I could picture the interior of the Twin Towers as I'd last seen it just two months earlier when I was there—tall, expansive, and bustling with crowds of people.

After about 15 minutes, I realized CNN was broadcasting the same images over and over again, and there was little conclusive information about the attack. I felt the best thing to do was to pull my class together and leave the lecture hall, so I asked them to leave with me.

We went outside and assembled under a big oak tree. Struggling to remain calm and professional, I said, "I really don't have a good sense of what's going on at this point, but it's upsetting to us all, so let's have a short class and go do what we need to do. I have friends and family in the New York City area so I want to make sure they're okay as soon as possible."

They were quiet, and relieved, I believe, to return to a bit of the regular routine of class, although nothing about that day was really routine at all. They were stunned by the newscast, and fear permeated the time we spent together that day.

The next day, I had an 8 a.m. class. Everyone in the class looked tired, including me. The students wanted to talk about the attacks. Some students had friends and family in the military. We were all concerned. Some of the students wanted to go to New York City to help.

I sat and listened to their needs to do something concrete and meaningful. "How could I possibly continue teaching as if nothing had happened?"

We discussed the idea of doing something as a class to help, but we had no idea what to do. I said I'd call the local Red Cross chapter before our next class to see what we could do.

When I contacted the Red Cross later that day, they invited me to bring my class to their headquarters the following week and discuss possible class projects. They mentioned several ways that my students could help locally. I then coordinated the upcoming assignments with the possibilities they mentioned. This was all new to me, but it required the type of experiential, hands-on approach to learning that I valued, giving students concrete experience applying the course concepts as they executed a project in the community.

The service project was a great learning experience for the students. Based on the issues outlined by the director of the agency, the students worked in groups on projects that included a promotional plan for the chapter's fund drive, a strategic plan for involving more teenage volunteers, and a public relations plan for increasing involvement with local business and industry.

The student groups met with staff at the Red Cross several times throughout the semester. They presented their projects publicly to the Red Cross staff. The director of the local chapter responded with enthusiasm, gratitude, and abundant feedback to the students, asking their permission to follow through on the projects based on their work. That was a bigger reward than any grade I could give them, I realized. They had made a difference. They had learned. And, as a teacher, I had learned a great deal, too.

Reflect and respond. Consider what you have learned from the reflective process and how you use it to improve student learning. Look inward and recap your own reflections as you respond to the following questions from the Self quadrant of the The Engaged Teaching and Learning model.

- What brought you to teaching, and what keeps you teaching?
- What are your strengths and habits as a teacher?
- What do you need to change or learn to improve student learning?

Engaged Teaching Strategy 7a: Cell Phone Survey

Directions: If you have a cell phone policy, suspend it for a few minutes and ask students to take out their cell phones and send a text message question to five friends. Give the students a question to ask that is related to course content or learning, such as "What are the main sources of stress in your life right now?" (psychology course), "How often do you eat fast food each week?" (health/science course), or "What are your best strategies for succeeding in college?" (general learning question). Tally and discuss responses immediately in class if time permits. Or, ask students to summarize and bring responses to the next class period when you will debrief the process of collecting information electronically and how the information can be used. There are some free polling websites that many professors use in a similar fashion.

Expanded Engaged Teaching Strategy 7b: Anonymous Learning Audit

Directions: After a few weeks into the semester, ask students to respond in writing (anonymously and without discussion) to the following questions:

1) What does the teacher do that helps me learn in this class?
2) What things can the teacher change to improve learning in this class?
3) What things can the students do to improve learning in this class?

Allow about 10 minutes for students to finish writing. Ask for two or three volunteers to lead a class discussion about the questions while you leave the room. Instruct the volunteers to ask for student feedback to the questions and record responses on the board. Stress to the students that this process is anonymous and should include comments from as many students as possible (set the group discussion time frame for 12 to 15 minutes). When you return to the room, review the list and thank students for their input. If you need clarification on some of the comments and what they mean, ask students for feedback. You may extend the discussion at this point or come back to it at the next class meeting to explore how the suggestions can be used.

Part Three

Sustaining Engaged Teaching and Learning

Chapter Eight

Tools for Engaged Teaching

Teaching without learning is just talking.
> —Thomas Angelo and Patricia Cross

The mediocre teacher tells.
The good teacher explains.
The superior teacher demonstrates.
The great teacher inspires.
> —William Arthur Ward

Author Narrative: There's a Lot of Material to Cover

"We have a lot of material to cover today, class."

"Oh, no," we all groaned silently as we exchanged "we know what that means" glances at each other. Yes, we knew what we were in for: a lot of lecturing, listening, note taking, endless Power Point slides, and a very short break—a lot of telling.

We need a reason to learn. We need teachers who help us learn how to do things along with knowing things. We want teachers to be doers with us, not just tellers.

I wished that the teacher could help us to learn in an easier way—something like when my dad taught me to ride my first two-wheeled bike. I remember well how I learned that lesson. I was eight years old the summer I got a brand new pink and white Schwinn two-wheeled bike. Our driveway was gravel, which made it hard to ride a bike at all, much less a two-wheeled bike without training wheels. I spent all day long trying: a day of continually falling down and scraping up my knees. I was banged up and exhausted, but determined to ride my new bike that day. Then, my dad came home from work, and as he stepped down from his pick-up truck, I begged him to help me.

Dad said, "Get on the bike, Nanc. Hang on and pedal hard."

I did. I pedaled harder than ever, hearing the gravel crunch as I held tight to the handlebars to keep them straight. I could feel Dad's strong hands grasping the bottom of the seat below me as he guided me through the driveway, picking up the pace. I kept pedaling, harder and harder, squeezing the handlebars with all my might. It was so much easier with him helping me!

He guided me up and down the driveway a couple of times, working up a small dust storm of dirt and gravel. I was starting to get the hang of it, pedaling through the pain of my scraped and bruised knees. I was finally keeping the handlebars straight and pedaling at a steadier pace, when I realized he had let go!

I kept going and heard him laugh as he said, "There you go, Nanc! Keep pedaling!"

I did it!

I kept going, finally doing it for myself, yet knowing my dad was nearby in the driveway in case I fell. I was soon bicycling all over, riding down the road to visit my grandparents or friends, or just riding for the fun of it. I biked all summer, going places on my own, exploring the nearby country roads and pathways. I felt so free! So strong! Riding my new bike gave me an exhilarating sense of adventure and power. Dad helped me gain control over my new bike, and riding it nearly every day built my confidence and skill.

Likewise, teachers who support us or guide us as we learn help us as we struggle through the unfamiliar or uncomfortable. Teachers who actually have us do something, and help us do it initially, help us learn in a way that sticks.

Reflect and respond.

- What are some things you've recently learned that brought back earlier memories of learning something new? How did you learn then?
- What one area of teaching is most difficult for you? What would you like to learn about it to improve student learning?

- What one area of teaching and learning intrigues or interests you? What would you like to learn about that area?

Fifty Engaged Teaching Ideas and Strategies

I've asked students around the country to describe their good teachers to me. Some of them describe people who lecture all the time, some of them describe people who do little other than facilitate group process, and others describe everything in between. But all of them describe people who have some sort of connective capacity, who connect themselves to their students, their students to each other, and everyone to the subject being studied.

—Parker Palmer

Given that there is no one best way of teaching or guaranteed prescription for success, this chapter presents 50 ideas for engaged teaching and learning. Here you will find a wide variety of ideas and approaches from which you can choose what best

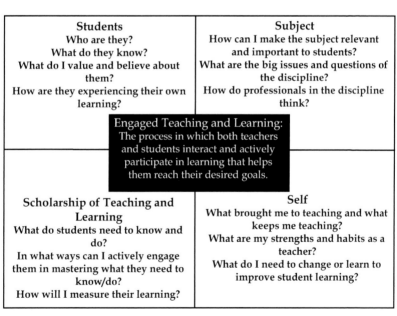

Students Who are they? What do they know? What do I value and believe about them? How are they experiencing their own learning?	Subject How can I make the subject relevant and important to students? What are the big issues and questions of the discipline? How do professionals in the discipline think?
Scholarship of Teaching and Learning What do students need to know and do? In what ways can I actively engage them in mastering what they need to know/do? How will I measure their learning?	Self What brought me to teaching and what keeps me teaching? What are my strengths and habits as a teacher? What do I need to change or learn to improve student learning?

Engaged Teaching and Learning: The process in which both teachers and students interact and actively participate in learning that helps them reach their desired goals.

Figure 6. The Model of Engaged Teaching and Learning, illustrating all four quadrants: Students, Subject, Scholarship of Teaching and Learning, and Self.

fits. These ideas emerged from the teachers and students surveyed for The Engaged Teacher Study as well as from the vast literature on teaching and learning. Some may be approaches that work for you now or have worked for you in the past; others may work for you in the future, some may never work for you at all. Teaching and learning are not exact sciences, but complex processes in which students and teachers interact through various approaches to mastering subjects. There are no absolute rights and wrongs in this process.

The Engaged Teacher Study has produced a model of Engaged Teaching and Learning and definition of "engaged teaching and learning": *The process in which both teachers and students interact and actively participate in learning that helps them reach their desired goals.*

The Model of Engaged Teaching and Learning (see Figure 6) illustrates how your knowledge and where you focus your energy informs your teaching practices. The quadrants or components of the model do change throughout your teaching career and the definition of engaged teaching and learning in your practice may change as well.

Keep in mind that no matter what you do or how you do it, you will never have complete control of the outcomes of student learning; there will always be factors such as students' home lives or their diligence that are out of your control. But, through your efforts as a teacher you can substantially enhance student learning and perhaps overcome some outside factors.

Students are the co-producers of learning, and you can help them take responsibility for their own learning. Sometimes the best you can do as an engaged teacher is what Barr and Tagg (1995) suggest: "create environments and experiences that bring students to discover and construct knowledge for themselves, to make students members of communities of learners that make discoveries and solve problems." (p. 4)

The following 50 suggestions are a variety of effective teaching ideas and strategies. They have been tested and used by the teachers included in this study. Pick some that fit your culture, appeal to your teaching style and, most importantly, are likely to help your students engage in deep, significant, and lasting learning.

1) **Make the first 15 minutes count.** Research on student impressions shows that in the first 15 minutes of class students typically form an impression of you as a teacher and what kind of experience they will have in your class (Povlacs, 1985). Do come to class prepared with information that the students need and use the first few minutes in class. Ways to do so include: pose an interesting question to spark discussion, ask students to write responses and compare in pairs, give a brief quiz over the assigned readings, or share relevant news about the subject and use it for discussion.

2) **Exude enthusiasm.** Studies show that instructors who make lasting impressions on students are those who display enthusiasm (McKeachie, 1998). Let your passion for your subject or teaching itself positively influence your students throughout the semester. Don't hide the fact that you enjoy your subject or what you are doing. Smile, develop your sense of humor and use it. Share cartoons and humorous anecdotes related to teaching, learning, technology, and your subject. But, never direct that humor or sarcasm directly at a student.

3) **Create an active, learning-centered environment based on brain-based research.** Use a variety of instructional methods. Be appropriately challenging yet supportive. Give students choices. Provide specific and learner controlled feedback. Stimulate emotions in positive ways. Trigger recall by association. Switch gears frequently. Provide students time to process. Make learning relevant. Build intrinsic motivation by using ground rules, feedback and promoting self-confidence in students. (Jensen, 2008)

4) **Be consistent.** Don't change course policies or rules mid-way through the semester (e.g., If you do not accept late work, then there is no late work). Get student work graded and back on a regular basis, preferably the next week. And, start and finish class on time every time you meet. Develop the habit of arriving a bit early and staying a few minutes after class to chat with students and answer questions. You will learn about students and their concerns, as well as build trust.

5) **Do something different.** Sit on your desk. Walk around the classroom. Use silence. Start the class with a thought-provoking question or surprising statement. Ask students to sit next

to someone they don't know. Switch modalities or use new media to introduce a new topic or concept. Whatever you do to add contrast or novelty, make sure that it has purpose and that you convey the intended purpose to students. Here is one way to do something different: add a twist to a class discussion, debate or writing exercise by first requiring students to take a written stance on a relevant issue and then ask students to defend the position opposite to their original stance. This could be in writing, in an impromptu debate, or general class discussion. This will engage students in critical thinking and help them see things from different perspectives.

6) **Create a classroom code of ethics to encourage civility and responsibility.** To encourage a positive learning environment and courteous interaction, have students discuss and create guidelines for student/faculty roles and responsibilities, civility guidelines, and ethical classroom practices. See Appendix D for examples.

7) **Take time to know students and treat them as unique individuals.** Granted, this is much more challenging in larger classes. Sometimes it is your tone of voice, using a student's name, or merely the fact that you take a few minutes with a student after class that communicates you value them. As one student commented: "The best teachers I've had treated me like I'm a unique individual, and not just another 7-digit student number on their class roster. They put in the extra time to figure out what it is about each student that makes them special. That might sound really cheesy, but it's a big deal from the student perspective. It makes you feel like you're worth their time."

8) **Take students out of their comfort zone.** Learning involves change, and students will typically resist discomfort. So, develop creative ways to stretch and challenge your students to apply subject matter and stretch beyond their current boundaries. Example: Ask them to imagine they were born the opposite gender and have them share how their experiences would be different. Discuss. One student commented, "I remember one professor specifically who used activities and assignments which took us out of our comfort zone to build camaraderie... What these activities did was take the class as

a whole and put us on the same level. Not only did it breed a team feeling, but empathy and compassion for others. All the walls that we had so carefully constructed came tumbling down, thus allowing the learning process to take hold."

9) **Display emotions appropriately.** Always be cool. Don't blow your top and display anger toward students. Handle emotional discipline issues professionally and privately when needed. If you need to, walk out of the classroom and collect yourself. If you're dealing with a disruptive student, ask them to step out of the classroom. A community college English major describes the effect an instructor's emotions had in the classroom: "I remember a day in Comp 111 class when my instructor read from an essay written by a former student. The essay was very personal and dealt with abuse. At a certain point, my instructor was moved so strongly that he started to cry in class. I didn't view it as a weakness at all, in fact that event showed me how much he cared and how strong he was to be able to share such a powerful piece of writing with us."

10) **Get students out of the classroom.** Keep in mind that the classroom is one context among many in which students learn. Meet in the library, coffee shop, or at a community site. Schedule a field trip or observation to a business, school, or non-profit agency. Use service-learning assignments, internships, field work, community research, or informational interviews that take students off campus. See Appendix C for service-learning ideas.

11) **Move students up the cognitive skill ladder.** As you create assignments, frame classroom discussions or formulate lectures or exam questions, consider the type of cognitive skills you're asking students to perform. Use writing-to-learn strategies to move students through the levels. Become familiar with Bloom's *Taxonomy of Educational Objectives: Handbook I, Cognitive Domain* (1956) that explains following cognitive skills that aid with learning:

- Recall—students remember when you ask them to define, describe or list.
- Understand—students grasp meaning when you ask them to discuss, explain, or classify.

- Apply—students solve problems when you ask them to use, illustrate, demonstrate, or apply.
- Analyze—students understand when you ask them to compare, contrast, or criticize.
- Synthesize—students combine ideas to form a new whole when you ask them to create, design, or compose.
- Evaluate—students make value judgments when you ask them to argue, assess, recommend, or discuss.

12) **Conduct classroom research.** There are many types of classroom research and tools, like the Minute Paper, Muddiest Point, and Background Knowledge Probe (Angelo & Cross, 1993). Brookfield's (2006) Critical Incident Questionnaire includes questions such as "When did you feel most engaged in class? Least engaged? What was the most important thing you learned today? What is not clear? What questions remain as you leave class today? What did the teacher do that helped, or did not help, you learn?" You can use results to make adjustments to improve student learning. See Appendix B for an example.

13) **Ask questions skillfully to elicit responses.** Ask questions periodically, as appropriate, to see if students are making sense of the material. Learn how to ask questions skillfully in ways that invite student response and help them save face if they do not know the "answer." The question NOT to ask is "Are there any questions?" This leads students to respond with a "yes" or "no" closed answer and can shut down discussion. Unintentionally, it may even intimidate shy or confused students into deeper silence. A better way is to say, "I usually get a question or two about this . . . now, what are your questions or comments?" You may want to end class with a question such as, "What one thing will you do next week to enhance your own learning about the subject?" or "What questions remain about what we covered today?" Ask students to write responses anonymously and turn in. Start the next class by sharing questions and feedback from students. When a student asks you a question in class, repeat or paraphrase the question to make sure other students hear it and that you understand it. Once you get students geared up to participate, try some advanced strategies, such as relaying

the question back to the class and waiting for them to answer it. If you grade on class discussion and participation, explain how you expect students to participate, how often, and how you will grade them on their participation.

14) **Show students how to use their notes.** Ask students to refer to the notes they've been taking in class (be sure that you have built an expectation and format for note-taking into your classroom culture and syllabus) and say, "Now, based on what I've just said and what you've jotted down in your notes, what are your questions or comments?" Then, just stop talking. Use silence and engaging eye contact to encourage students to speak up. They will if you just wait long enough.

15) **Things to do on the first day**.

- Introduce the course subject matter in an interesting way and build a case for learning by explaining to students what positive advantages learning the subject matter will produce in their lives. Make your remarks student-centered and phrased as promises: "When you have completed this course, you will be able to..." To interest and motivate students, use wording like "challenging and invigorating" when describing difficult assignments.

- Discover and relate students' prior knowledge about the subject to enhance learning connections. Bring in former students to talk about how to succeed in the course.

- Model and facilitate student participation to set the tone for future course expectations. Ask students to introduce themselves or each other in pairs or groups. Use simple questions such as, "Tell us what you do" and "What do you expect to learn in this course?" Have students collaboratively generate guidelines for positive learning in the class or a classroom code of ethical conduct (see Appendix D for examples). Ask students to exchange contact information with another student or two with whom they can compare notes, study, or who can fill them in if they miss a class. Collect necessary student information for your purposes; see Appendix L for sample form.

- Have students review the syllabus in groups and develop three or four questions about the requirements, grading, course policies and procedures, your availability, or anything else they need to know or find unclear. There are plenty of excellent resources on how to construct a good syllabus (Filene, 2005; Lang, 2008). In both your syllabus and during the first class meeting, you should discuss your availability, best way to contact you, and when (office hours, "virtual" online hours, when you check email, response time, etc.).

- Ask students what they want, need and expect to learn in the course, and how they learn best. Have them set goals and revisit them throughout the term.

16) **Preview, review, and "hook" students at the beginning and end of each class.** Begin and end each class with a hook during the first and last 10 minutes, giving them a good reason to get engaged and a good reason to come back. Also, sandwich your class time between a helpful preview at the beginning and review at the end to recap learning. Ask students to conduct the review. If necessary, add anything they missed that is important to you.

17) **Find out what students know.** To check students' prior knowledge about the subject, use the widely adapted instrument, the Background Knowledge Probe (Angelo & Cross, 1993). Research generally shows that how much students learn is to a large extent determined by what prior knowledge they have about a subject.

18) **Engage students in critical thinking through discussion/ debate.** Have students bring in two quotes from a homework reading assignment, one they support and one they could argue. Set up debate groups based on their choices and peer evaluation for groups. Refer to the work of Richard Paul for ideas on using the Socratic method for teaching critical thinking and reasoning in the classroom.

19) **Build credibility.** Credibility with students is not automatic. It must be earned, especially with today's Millennial students. Research on credibility in the classroom shows that it "is largely gained or lost on the basis of whether you show respect for the students, an interest in their learning, and a commitment to following the policies you outlined in the syllabus." (Huston, 2009, p. 84)

20) **Recognize differences in online teaching and learning.** When teaching online courses, timely individual feedback and a strong social presence of the teacher in cyberspace are crucial. Brookfield (2006) found teacher responsiveness as "the most important factor contributing to the success of a discussion-based, online class." (pp. 198-199) He suggests teachers make the frequency of their participation (e.g., when you are available and the turnaround time for email responses and grading) explicit when the class begins so students know what to expect (p. 201). Some additional suggestions for teaching online include:
- Take an online course or training first before you attempt to teach online.
- Look at the learner/student view when you teach online.
- Look at courses taught by faculty with extensive experience and expertise teaching online.
- Research how students are learning just as you would in a regular class.
- Discuss issues and concerns with colleagues who also teach online courses.

21) **Increase student responsibility for learning.** Create conditions and practices to help students understand their responsibility for learning. Define what your policies and consequences are and hold students to them: participation guidelines, late work, expectations for group members, required supplies, reading the text, and the like. Ask student to identify what they are doing that contributes to their learning success.

22) **Tell students why, not just what.** Remember that students want to know how whatever they are being asked to know or do is important and necessary to their personal, intellectual, or occupational development. Tell them. A philosophy teacher explains, "Also, tell them *why* they are doing whatever: Why are we doing groups? Why are we doing debates? Explain your purposes and aims of the activity and *how* it is supposed to work. Students appreciate knowing these things and give activities more of a chance if they do." (R. Forsberg, personal communication, July 17, 2010)

23) **Model engagement.** You, the teacher, must model initial engagement in the learning activity required, especially when

it involves risk, humiliation, or potential embarrassment. Model the positive engagement behaviors you expect students to use when you speak, demonstrate, answer questions, and respond to students. Do the exercise yourself and show students your finished result, explain what you thought and did when working on it.

24) **Require students to call you.** Yes, you read that correctly. Today's students prefer texting to talking, and this change minimizes the development of essential skills, such as how to interpret cues from vocal intonations. Here is how I used the telephone to connect with students, increase retention, and provide feedback: After a few years of a dismal completion rate with one of my distance courses (I met with the students once a month and conducted the rest of the class through an online course management system), I changed things with a simple phone call.

I required the students to call me at designated times between the first and second class meetings, the time when most students dropped out or stopped doing the course work. I told them I would then give each of them a question from the required reading for that week. Then, while still on the phone, without notes or preparation, they would have to talk for one to two minutes. As they spoke, I made copious notes of their strengths and weaknesses in speaking (vocal), organization, and critical thinking. I then gave them my verbal assessment, always making a point to start with something positive before sharing suggestions for improvement. Finally, we talked about their first graded assignments due the next class meeting.

Results: The students were given "ungraded" feedback (with participation points for calling in on time) plus an opportunity to talk about their upcoming assignments, forcing them to think, ask questions, and respond to questions. This opened the door for continued two-way communication throughout the semester. The completion rate shot up dramatically for the course from approximately 60% to 95%. Moreover, their improvement in mastery of course outcomes and critical thinking was equally dramatic.

25) Talk less. If you find yourself doing most of the talking, you are probably working too hard. According to research (Boice, 1996), if you increase student involvement in discussions you will increase the learning that goes on, the approval ratings students give, and the satisfaction of teaching that comes with creating connections. Monitor the amount of talking and learning in discussions.

26) Learn students' names and faces. Use name cards, memory techniques, or a seating chart to help you with student names early in the semester. One instructor took a group photograph of the class and uploaded it to the course management site home page (with permission from the students) to help students remember names and faces, too. This also works well for a strictly online course if your course management system allows students to post their photo to the class list.

27) Shake hands with students on the last day of class. Here is how a student described a memorable moment on the last day of class:

> I will never forget the last day of class with this teacher because it makes me sad to be done with the class, knowing how great of a teacher I had. I remember shaking their hand and getting emotional because when you're in college you always have a few 'bad' teachers, and it makes you more grateful when you have a great one. Great teachers change your life.

28) Practice learner-centered teaching. Read Weimer's *Learner-Centered Teaching: Five Key Changes to Practice* (2002), and apply her suggestions, which include focusing on the following five areas: (1) what the student is learning, (2) how the student is learning, (3) the conditions under which the student is learning, (4) whether the student is retaining and applying the learning, and (5) how current learning positions the student for future learning.

29) Think-Write Pair-Share Variations. This is an effective technique to generate individual and group critical thinking plus increase participation. Pose a question to the class and instruct students to think and write individually for a few minutes. Then, ask students to share their answers with a partner for a few minutes. Finally, call on specific pairs to share their points in a class discussion.

30) **Use groups.** If you are using collaborative or cooperative learning strategies for graded assignments, consider strategically forming the groups yourself based on several factors, including student ability, diversity, personality, learning styles, and interest. Refer to Cooper and Robinson's (2011) volume of articles on the research and practice of small group learning or the recent work by Millis (2010). See sample Group Project Activity Log in Appendix M.

31) **Fishbowl discussion.** This is an effective technique to involve the entire class and generate dynamic group involvement. Give students a topic or problem to discuss and ask four or five students to sit in a circle and have a discussion (fish). The remaining students act as observers, seated in an outer circle around the small group in the center (bowl). The student observers take notes while watching and follow up with questions directed to the group in the fishbowl. Or, you can allow students to switch from the outer circle to the inner circle to participate in the discussion. Make sure your learning goals are clear to students for this activity and ask for volunteers (or draft uninhibited students into participating). In addition, become familiar with this learning activity and the expert debriefing required by you to make the learning transparent.

32) **Stand up steps re-order.** Present a series of steps in a mixed order and form groups with the same number of students as the number of steps. Have students re-order the steps correctly in their groups by standing up in order of the steps and reporting out, one group at a time. Discuss similarities and differences.

33) **Use a failure-proof task.** Design a subject-related failure-proof task for students to complete early in the semester, preferably in the first class meeting if possible. Research shows an early experience of unexpected success can reduce the level of student resistance with the learning process. For instance, ask students to introduce each other or describe their experience with the subject.

34) **Try a little small talk.** Greet your students before class starts as they enter the classroom. Ask them how their day is going. This only works if you are genuine when you ask. It makes students feel like you really do care about them. Sincerely

compliment them or make a comment: "Thanks for coming to class early . . . I like the color of your laptop . . . Looks like you're having a busy day . . .That was quite a downpour this morning, wasn't it?"

35) **Use a variety of examples and teaching modalities.** Regular use of a variety teaching approaches and examples, anecdotes, video clips, and autobiographical illustrations is strongly appreciated by students. Many students prefer to learn from "stories," and research confirms the effectiveness of stories on listener retention. Many instructors note that using personal anecdotes lets students know how active and experienced the instructor is in their field. "He/she's done it! He/she knows his/her stuff!" are frequently found in student evaluations for teachers who do this.

36) **DWYSYWD (Do What You Say You Will Do).** Effective ways to build credibility and rapport with students include showing up early to class, knowing the text, explaining subject and expectations clearly, asking students if they understand, answering students' questions, following the syllabus (especially adhering to your own course policies), reminding students of upcoming deadlines and due dates, and always *do what you say you will do.* Use frequent previews and reminders in emails and announcements, especially if you are teaching online. If you have a late policy, follow it. If you require homework to be word-processed, only accept it word-processed. If you say you will have work graded by a specific date, do it. In other words, do what you say you will do.

37) **Make a fabulous first impression.** Make sure you make a great first impression! It is true that you never get a second chance to make a first impression. First impressions are very important and have a great influence on what students conclude about us as teachers. This is the case even in the face of later, contradicting evidence. Research psychologists confirm that once people develop a belief, those beliefs are extremely resistant to change. In fact, people are more likely to interpret ambiguous new information in favor of their initial beliefs. If you make a positive first impression with your students, they are more likely to rationalize away your not-so-great moments in the future. Frame your authority by the way you

introduce yourself, the way you speak and appear, and the relevant information you share with students.

38) **Check understanding frequently.** Research indicates that students pay attention in much shorter chunks of time than we previously assumed, especially if we are lecturing. To stimulate attention you can interject questions, use writing-to-learn techniques, or conduct short classroom assessments every 15 to 20 minutes.

39) **Periodically assess for feedback on learning.** Frequently ask students to anonymously comment (in writing) on What helps me learn in this course? What hinders my learning? and What changes could be made — by me or by my instructor — to help me learn? Share the feedback with the students and discuss ways to increase learning.

40) **Suggestion box.** Use a suggestion box in your classroom or near your office, or use an electronic version to gather student feedback.

41) **Let students define parts of the learning.** In groups, have students generate a list of responses to relevant teaching/learning questions such as, What do effective teachers do in the classroom to help students learn? What kinds of assignments help you apply what you are learning? Have the student groups share their lists. At the end of class, ask students to anonymously write down one or two suggestions for improving the class based on the discussion. I call these "no name" feedback cards, using 3 x 5 index cards for these brief writing exercises. Share the feedback at the next class meeting. Thank them for their suggestions, and discuss how you will incorporate some of them.

42) **Use learning notes.** Show students how to use note-taking strategies to enhance learning. Instruct students to draw a line down the middle of a sheet of paper and label one side "Understood" and the other side "Unclear." Ask students to jot down notes regarding assignments, readings, lectures, etc. Take frequent 5 to 10 minute "time outs" to pair or group students. Instruct them to share their notes in small groups, working together to clear up the unclear side. Follow up with class discussion to further clarify issues and questions.

43) On the spot check. During class, ask yourself, "What's happening in my classroom? What I expected, or not?" Adjust if necessary. After class, ask yourself, "Based on what I noticed today, what needs to happen to enhance student learning?"

44) Pause. When asking questions, pause. Make strong and sustained eye contact with students. Silently count to 10 before moving on. Don't answer your own questions if no one else does. Pair or group students to discuss answers.

45) Teach to the Millennial learner. Consider what we know about Millennials: they are comfortable with and connected through technology, racially and ethnically diverse, civic-minded, interested in doing, achieving, impatient, team-oriented, and closer to their parents than previous generations (Howe & Strauss, 2000). Based on research aimed at teaching and learning for the Millennials, consider the following approaches:

- Use media and visual images students recognize (news sources, TV shows).
- Use technology and use it well; stay connected through technology and be clear about your online availability (when you check email and how frequently).
- Use active-learning and cooperative group learning (service-learning, games, projects) to effectively create a community of engaged learners.
- Provide clear instructions and expectations (both what you expect of students and what they can expect of you), demonstrate respect, and provide abundant and explicit feedback to establish credibility.

46) Break. Take frequent breaks. Consider the ebb and flow of students' energy levels during a class period. Try to balance intense periods with calm periods. This is even more important in a three-hour class session than in 50-minute sessions.

47) Set goals. Always set clear goals for classes. Ask yourself, "What do I want students to learn?" Throughout the semester, ask yourself, "Why am I doing this?" Ask students to set learning goals at the beginning of the class, collect them, and refer to them throughout the semester to help students analyze their learning experiences.

48) Learn how students learn best. Consider the research and assessments on learning and use it to help students understand how they learn and how to best study based on their preferred approach. Several learning inventories are available and can be scored online; your college learning center should have a variety of resources available, too. One student described how her truly good teachers do this, stating:

> They learn about you and learn how you learn best. I had a teacher that took the time to get to know her students good enough to know who was a visual learner, or who works better in groups, etc. Then when you were struggling with something she knew just how to help. The best teachers engage students individually so they can be the best they are capable of.

49) Don't try to rescue your students. Experiencing an unfortunate crisis is understandable and may require compassion or leeway, but trying to "save" a student in a jam because of their own lack of planning or effort sends a message to students that they don't need to be responsible for their own learning. They do. Learning requires responsibility both on the part of the learner as well as the teacher. The teacher sets the tone initially for creating a positive classroom environment, but it requires responsibility on the part of both teachers and students to maintain positive learning experiences.

50) Daily, ask yourself these questions.

- Why do I do what I do? What's working well? And, not so well?
- What backgrounds do students bring to the class and how can they use these? How can I use the knowledge to enrich the learning in the class?
- What do I know about today's students and the nature of learning that will help me engage them in learning?
- How can I engage students and help motivate them to learn?
- What challenges can I create for students to lead them into deep, sustained, and significant learning?
- How can I help develop a community of responsible learners with my students?

Summary

There you have it: 50 strategies engaged teachers use to help students learn. There is no one best practice that emerged from the literature or from The Engaged Teacher Study. This chapter contains several ideas and strategies, and you may find many of them useful in your teaching practice.

Author Narrative: What I Remember

The teachers I remember learning the most from are the ones who remain vivid in my memory and have influenced my own teaching practice. Although I can't remember exactly what they said, I distinctly remember how they made me feel: valued, significant, unique, worthy and capable of learning. They taught me about life and they gave me hope.

I felt those "aha" moments in their classes. I left with my mind buzzing with exciting questions and ideas. They didn't "give" me answers; they taught me how to think, question, and seek meaning that I can apply in my life. So many of those learning connections resound in my life each day, confirming that, indeed, I did learn.

Reflect and respond. As you examine the ideas in this chapter and decide which ones you may want to use, consider these questions:

- Looking over the 50 ideas listed in this chapter, which ones would you like to try?
- How will you assess the effectiveness of the new approaches that you try?

Engaged Teaching Strategy 8a: Reflection Letter to Future Students

Directions: Near the end of the semester, have students write a "Reflection Letter to the Future Students." Specify the questions you want them to answer in the letter and what you will do with it. The letter helps students reflect on their own learning and provides you feedback on your teaching. It can also be used to introduce the class to students in future semesters. Questions to ask might include:

- How would you describe this course to a friend about to enroll in this course next semester?

- What advice would you give future students to help them do well in this course?
- How has this course helped you?
- What helped you learn in this course?
- What suggestions do you have to improve this course?
- What are the three or four most important things you've learned in this course that you think you will remember five years from now?
- Anything else? (feedback, comments, suggestions, etc.)

Expanded Engaged Teaching Strategy 8b: Student Timeline

Directions: On the last day of class, demonstrate how students can construct a timeline of their life. As you demonstrate on the board, ask students to draw a horizontal line on a sheet of paper. Ask them to insert the year they were born on the far left side of the line and the year they think they will die on the far right of the line. Show them how to place today's date in a spot on the line based the ratio of their years of life so far and their projected years until death. Model how to place dates on the line between their birth date and the present to represent significant times in their life (achievements, obstacles, transitions, etc.). Finally, ask them to project ahead into the "wet cement" future of their life and forecast what is to come. Ask them to fill in goals they hope to achieve and projected milestones in the future by listing them and the projected dates to the right of the date they are constructing the timeline. Provide envelopes and ask students to write their name and the address to which they'd like their timeline sent in one year. Follow up by sending them to students a year later.

Chapter Nine

Building a Community of Engaged Teachers

How do we find solutions to the problems we face engaging students in learning? Most likely from our own creative ideas or by talking to colleagues or by looking to the literature. . . . the seeds of solutions to even the most complicated student engagement problems abound in the ideas we find in workshops, conversations with colleagues, and the good practice literature.

— Elizabeth Barkley

Author Narrative: Marathon Teacher

When I ran a marathon I had no idea how much it was like teaching. I made the connection between the two unlikely experiences after I had been teaching for a few years. It was during a particularly rough semester when the similarities between teaching and running crystallized in ways that have stuck with me.

A marathon is 26.2 miles long. I teach at a college where the semesters are 15 weeks long. Months of preparation, training, and building endurance are what helped me successfully finish the marathon. To do well as a teacher, I spend months developing new courses, improving current courses, reading literature on pedagogy, talking to colleagues, and engaging in professional development and coursework. Both training for a marathon and for good teaching require a routine of consistent physical and mental training. When I ran the marathon, my physical and mental training paid off so I was able to stay at a steady pace and stay focused on the goal of finishing the race. I never considered quitting. As a teacher, I constantly prepare, study, and engage in my subject to set the pace for student learning.

Most marathon courses are full of turns and hills and stretches of flat land and some random potholes and speed bumps that force runners to pay attention and stay focused. Likewise, a semester is full of peaks and valleys and stretches of not knowing exactly what's coming next. Yet, you know you have to remain focused as a teacher and pay attention to what students learn and don't learn so well. Both require endurance, training, and focus in order to finish. And every mile in a marathon, just like every day I walk into the classroom, is a little bit different.

Throughout the training, mentors are important as they model desirable behaviors and support our development. Becoming a runner, especially a marathon runner, requires the guidance of a mentor. Likewise, when we first begin to teach, our teaching practice is typically modeled after our mentors and the good teachers we witnessed ourselves. And, we need them for support and feedback throughout our teaching careers.

Reflect and respond.
- What are your strengths and weaknesses as a teacher?
- What challenges or "speed bumps" have you encountered as a teacher?
- How do you "train" as a teacher? How do you maintain "balance?"
- Describe the support you've received from your mentors and colleagues. How has it helped you throughout the stages of your teaching career?

Building a Community of Engaged Teachers

Crowded college classrooms, reduced resources, less time for professional development, increased proportions of adjunct faculty, and growth in online teaching have made isolation and disengagement among teachers more prevalent. The solitude and autonomy of the traditional teaching life does not encourage reflective practices such as sharing teaching ideas and materials with colleagues, seeking feedback, team teaching, and discussing student learning. Lack of reflective practice promotes isolation.

In an essay entitled, "Responsibilities of a College Teacher," Rojek (2001) addresses some of these issues. He recommends that both new and veteran instructors sit in on each other's classes, making teaching more public and facilitating examination of teaching practices. He comments:

> We desperately need more collegial exchanges, formal and informal, about classroom techniques and teaching strategies. I am embarrassed to say that I have visited very few classes taught by my colleagues, and very few of my colleagues have ever visited my classroom. There is very little sharing of teaching methods, and yet teaching is our profession. (p. 50)

Not making our teaching public can easily cause us to lose sight of our strengths and weaknesses as teachers. The problem created by this lack of transparency is described by Brookfield (2006): "College teachers spend so much time teaching behind the closed doors of their classrooms that this isolation can induce them into a distorted perception of their own failings" (p. 260). As noted by Weimer (2002), instructional quality suffers as a consequence of professional isolation. Assessing our teaching is as important as assessing student learning. Weimer recommends:

> We need to engage colleagues in efforts to understand and improve instruction. To begin, quite simply, we need to engage our colleagues in meaningful intellectually robust conversations about teaching and learning. . . . Whatever the vehicle, we use conversations with colleagues to test the assumptions and premises on which our educational practice rests. (pp.119-120)

What appears to be lacking among teaching colleagues is exactly what exemplary teachers are noted for doing, according to Boice (1996). He cites the following as practices of exemplary teachers:
- They collaborate more with other teachers.
- They share teaching ideas, assignments, and presentations.
- They encourage more observation and feedback of their work.
- They join in interdisciplinary conversations about teaching and learning.
- They observe and learn from other exemplars.

Just as students need opportunities to develop relationships with other students, so do teachers. Likewise, just as learning is about making connections, so is teaching. Teachers need time, encouragement, and structure to develop significant collegial relationships with other teachers. Real and sustained improvements happen in purposeful communities of teachers learning from each other.

Collegiality is crucial for all faculty members. Meaningful collegiality includes

- Sharing advice and ideas
- Observing each other (not just at promotion time)
- Nominating colleagues for opportunities and awards
- Taking a sincere interest in the development of colleagues

Whether faculty members are involved in formal mentor relationships or merely sharing ideas in the coffee room, collegiality provides a buffer and a springboard for developing, refining, and revising our teaching practices.

Overcoming Challenges to Collegiality and Community

Perhaps the thought of all of this inner investigation of your teaching life overwhelms you. You may feel like you need a sabbatical to reflect on all the questions and try the suggestions posed in this chapter. Maybe you feel like you don't have the time to join a teaching circle to talk about teaching and learning or engage in professional development. But, a key to understanding what shapes and informs your teaching is taking the time to examine what you do through discussion, observation, and professional growth.

How can we create opportunities for faculty members to engage in meaningful discussions and assessments to help improve teaching and learning? Part of the answer lies in creating communities for teacher-learners who want to learn to teach in ways that research says actually works with students. Communities of teacher-learners, working within a shared educational culture that values teaching and learning above all else, provide support, information, and create networks for improved teaching and learning.

The development of faculty learning communities has grown

from faculty members' desire for community and support for investigation and implementation of new teaching and learning approaches and opportunities. Evidence shows that such learning communities increase interest in teaching and learning by providing safety and support for faculty to investigate, attempt, assess, and adopt new teaching and learning methods. Research shows faculty learning communities have proven to be effective for preparing new faculty and reinvigorating senior faculty, implementing new courses and curricula, and addressing institutional challenges (Cox, 2004). Model faculty learning community programs are part of the culture at many schools, including Miami University of Ohio and The Community College of Baltimore County.

Changes in Teaching Demand New Skills

One aspect of teaching that has greatly changed, especially at community colleges, is the increased demand for online course delivery. Many more teachers are teaching online. This increase in online teaching has required teachers to invest in skill development and master new technologies. Here is a seasoned faculty member's journey from the classroom to online teaching.

Teacher Snapshot: From Skeptical to Skilled

I was both skeptical and curious when my college encouraged faculty to offer online courses. I was resistant to convert any of my face-to-face classes to an online format, as I was sure it would diminish the integrity and rigor of the learning experience. I was convinced the online delivery mode would compromise significant student engagement. So, I enrolled in a professional development course for online teaching taught by the online faculty guru at my college. After I completed the training course, I taught my first online course, with the constant support and guidance of my faculty colleagues who also taught online.

That was seven years ago, and today I teach several courses online. My journey to the world of online teaching has not been easy, but it has made me much more aware of many aspects of teaching that we take for granted in face-to-face courses. I've learned how much more important timely communication, feedback, and thoroughly explained assignments are to online students. Some things that seem insignificant, like always using a student's name in an email or empathizing when students have technology issues, are very important when teaching online in order to create a responsive presence. I am sometimes overwhelmed with the amount of work and time it requires. I am constantly striving to improve both the process and content aspects of my online courses. I've developed active and assessable assignments for my online students that take them out into the field or their communities to apply course concepts.

I've learned to use discussion boards to build "community" and encourage student dialogue about the text. Discussion boards equalize participation because students can participate anytime, at their own pace. This may not be the case in regular classes because some students need more time to process before they think, speak, or write. Or, they are just shy or lack the self-confidence to speak up in class. Teaching an online class is different, but I have found that interaction and learning need not be comprised as I once thought.

Through numerous technology workshops taught by my colleagues, I continually improve my online courses. I've learned to use aspects of technology to personalize the class and embed related video clips, credible web sites, relevant news articles, and course supplement sites that enhance student engagement. I include a photograph of myself and a bit of personal information in the course syllabus (my educational background, hobbies, books I recommend). Since I started doing this a couple of years ago, I've noticed two differences: students use a more conversational tone to me in emails and I receive more emails from students. Sometimes a student on campus will walk up to me and tell me that I am their online teacher—they recognized me from the photograph in my syllabus!

Teaching online has forced me to become a better teacher because I have to continuously examine how to effectively engage students in learning online. So many students sign up because they think it will be less demanding of their time and less work than a face-to-face class. Many students are not only underprepared for college, but lack the skills to succeed in an online format. I've learned that timely communication and a strong teacher presence through lots of participation are essential: emails, announcements, participating in discussion boards, getting frequent feedback and grade updates to students. My advice to teachers contemplating teaching online:

Take an online course first before you attempt to teach online. Try to take one taught by a highly-regarded, veteran, online teacher. Go into the course site of a colleague's online course (with their permission). Take training courses taught online at your college. Talk to colleagues who also teach online. When you do teach online, look at the learner/student view so you can see exactly what students are seeing and experiencing. Good luck.

Tools for Reflection and Self-Appraisal/Assessment

One of the characteristics frequently mentioned by the teachers responding to The Engaged Teacher Survey was the habit of continual self-appraisal and reflection. Many of the teachers sought feedback from teaching colleagues and supervisors as well as from students. Some reflected on the culture and climate of their institutions as well. As a result of The Engaged Teacher Project, four instruments based on some of the work by Buckingham and Coffman (1999) have been developed as tools for faculty reflection and self-appraisal. They are included in the in the Appendix section of this book. They are:

- The Engaged Student Questionnaire (Appendix F)
- The Engaged Teacher Institutional Culture Questionnaire (Appendix G)
- The Engaged Teacher Colleague/Supervisor Questionnaire (Appendix H)
- The Engaged Teacher Instructor Self-Reflection Questionnaire (Appendix I)

Another helpful approach to self-appraisal when using the Engaged Student Questionnaire is to invite a colleague into your classroom to administer the instrument and tally the results for you. Follow up with a conversation, asking for your colleague's feedback and suggestions based on the student responses. Reflect on what you discover and make appropriate adjustments to your teaching practice.

Here is a look at how one teacher ended his teaching career as he took a reflective stance toward himself, his students, his subject, and teaching with his "Last Lecture." As a teacher of philosophy, he tries to model what a philosopher is, communicate clearly, share his passion for the subject, and stimulate students into being more than they are now by instilling an obsession with knowledge and character. He uses discussion and interaction, a la Socrates, believing students can leave his class thinking more clearly and critically than when they entered.

The day I visited his class was officially his last class as professor of philosophy at our college, as he was retiring at the end of the term. Given his low-keyed manner, my faculty colleagues and I were surprised when he sent us an email inviting us to what he entitled, "My Last Lecture." No, he was not dying, he informed us during the introduction of the lecture. He told us he simply wanted to share what he considered his seminal work as a teacher: his "What is the Meaning of Life?" lecture, which was delivered during the last meeting of his Introductory Philosophy course, his last class of the semester.

This is what he says he believes:

Teacher Snapshot: Getting Students to Think

Students are willing to learn and want to learn, but have been conditioned to expect less—that is, they have been rewarded for less than their best . . . students must be self-motivated to get the most out of any class or from any teacher. I have had numerous students tell me that they have never had to think about things or issues in more than one way. They tell me that they get confused, their heads hurt, and then clarity breaks through. The whole idea that thinking is tough and painful is a theme that has run-through my 36 years of teaching. What can be better than 'My head hurt, I was pushed to think, and then I did well on the test?'

Twenty-five Collaborative Strategies and Ideas for Engaged Teaching and Learning

Why wait until your "last lecture" to share what you do with your fellow teachers? You can begin now by starting with any one thing that involves the participation of at least one other person. It may be inviting colleagues into your classroom to listen and offer some feedback, or it may be something completely different. The following 25 suggestions are tools to improve teaching effectiveness that involve colleagues, mentors, etc. Pick what fits your culture, teaching style, and most importantly, helps improve the degree to which you engage students in deep, significant, and lasting learning:

1) **Participate in faculty teaching circles or faculty learning communities.** Teaching circles are informal, regular discussions among colleagues who share common concerns related to teaching and are driven by the membership of the circle. You decide on an issue as a group, such as teaching online, plagiarism, or student preparedness. Faculty learning communities are more structured and typically last a semester or two, are comprised of faculty from different disciplines, and focus on teaching issues, learning, and pedagogies (Cox, 2004). These groups help faculty learn from each other, generate and share ideas related to teaching and learning, offer resolutions to problems, and support each other.

2) **Enroll in a class.** Enroll in a class taught by a colleague outside your discipline to experience your own learning and how others teach.

3) **Observe yourself.** Videotape yourself teaching and yes, watch it. There is nothing like watching an actual video of *you* to spark self-awareness, in-depth reflection and appraisal. If you are brave, ask a colleague to watch it and give you comments, too.

4) **Ask yourself some key questions.** We teach students how to ask questions but how often do we ask ourselves important questions? Here are some key questions, suggested by Fish (1996), that we should be asking ourselves and discussing with our colleagues:

   • What activities in teaching give me the greatest satisfaction? What causes me to come away from a class feeling really high?

   • What do I do that seems to produce good responses in students—not just positive comments but eager attention, intelligent questions, and desire to engage in the material?

   • What modifications can I make in my teaching in order to increase the frequency of the wonderful moments referred to above?

   • If I had the power (without constraints . . .) to make three changes in my teaching and professional activities, what would they be?

- If I could communicate only five concepts, principles, and values to my students, what would they be?
- If I were to present my very last lecture to students . . . what would it contain?
- What three questions about teaching and teachers do *I* think are the most important to ask and have answered? (p. 143-145)

5) **Co-author or co-present with students or colleagues.** Some conferences and publications solicit work co-produced by faculty and students; choose one and make a presentation along with one or more of your students. This gives students solid publication and presentation experience. Plus, it is a great way to mentor students within your discipline or learn from colleagues.

6) **Bring a colleague to class.** Invite a colleague—one that will be least intimidating and most helpful—to your class to observe you teach. Let students know you are doing this to help improve learning in your classroom. Ask for a written observation, or take a short break halfway through the class to briefly discuss their observations. Or, sit down with them sometime soon after class and go over their observations and suggestions. Make adjustments. Thank them.

7) **Start a faculty book circle.** Select a book and get faculty members together for discussion, perhaps off campus. Focus on book selections that relate to learning and can be applied to all disciplines. Check to see if your dean or faculty support center will provide funds to purchase books based on faculty interest. Twenge's *Generation Me* (2006) or Huston's (2009) *Teaching What You Don't Know* cover a range of topics related to changes in today's students. Some other suggestions for a short-term or one-time discussion are to circulate an article from *The Chronicle of Higher Education* (the *Career* pages contain a column on teaching and essays on the academic life), the *College Teaching* journal, the *National Teaching and Learning Forum, The Teaching Professor,* or visit your Center for Teaching Excellence/Teaching and Learning for resources, training, books, articles, and websites, usually with links to resources on teaching and learning.

8) **Network and find a mentor.** Get out of your office and meet other faculty. Drop by their office during office hours (they are probably alone). Ask a faculty member you admire to be your mentor and schedule time with them.

9) **Stay "in love" with teaching and learning.** Good teachers often describe themselves as being in love with teaching, knowing how to weigh the delicate balance of listening and speaking, and knowing as much as possible the individual needs of students. Periodically, get together informally with colleagues to discuss the things you "love" about teaching and what's working well in your classroom.

10) **Create a learning community.** Create a community of learners by teaching with other faculty members in a fully integrated learning community, linked or team-taught course. The planning and collaboration with colleagues will provide meaningful opportunities to examine approaches to teaching and learning.

11) **Go public.** Make your teaching more public by inviting other classes, outside groups, your dean or president, and other colleagues into your classroom to attend capstone student presentations or to participate in class sessions.

12) **Get feedback.** Ask a colleague to do a Small Group Instructional Diagnosis or similar group feedback technique (Redmond & Clark, 1982; Angelo & Cross, 1993) around mid-semester. This will help you discover what students say helps them learn in the class, what needs improvement, and what specific suggestions students have for improving the course.

13) **Observe exemplary teachers.** Whenever you can, observe them, talk to them, study the ways they find success or failure, look at the ways they persist through obstacles and setbacks — and buy them lunch.

14) **Don't do it alone.** Seek out trusted peers for private and informal talks about concerning or troubling teaching situations. You may discover that your concerns are shared by them. This gives you an opportunity to talk about your frustrations, analyze solutions, and discover that you're not alone in your struggles. Knowing that your peers share some of the same difficulties may not provide immediate solutions but at least gives you relief by realizing you are not alone.

15) Learn something new outside of your comfort zone. Experience struggling as a learner yourself. Clumsy? Try a dance class. Mathematically challenged? Take a statistics class. Your experience will humble you and help you better relate to how students new to your discipline, or new to college, struggle when they learn something new. Take note of how you and others learn.

16) Make your teaching social. Become more public with your teaching by exchanging working teaching materials with a colleague for early/ongoing feedback (social partnership ensures timely completion), collaborating in classroom teaching, observing each other's classes, and joining in conversations with teachers working on courses like your own.

17) Float ideas. Ask a trusted colleague or two to listen to a bit of a lecture plan or exercise before trying it. Open your work up to feedback from peers, not just from your students. Make the content of teaching public, even before you think it is fully worthy.

18) Try some service-learning. Develop a service-learning project that links your course learning outcomes with relevant community-based experiences. Give students an audience wider than just one professor. Use pre- and post-reflection to tie it all together and to strengthen the learning. Grade for the amount and quality of learning, not for the amount of service hours (although you can set a minimum number of required service hours). See Appendix C.

19) Use teaching squares. Teaching squares are groups of four faculty members, from different disciplines, engaged in sharing what they do. They visit each other's classrooms, share teaching materials, reflect on classroom observations, and discuss reflections with colleagues. See Appendix K.

20) Apply for a sabbatical. Whether you get it or not, the process will help you crystallize some of the things you really want to develop as a teacher.

21) Learn about another field. Go to a conference in a field outside your own. See how you can apply what you learn to your teaching practice.

22) Visit your faculty center. If you have one, hang out at your faculty professional development center and check out the resources, courses, workshops, and assistance they offer. Discover opportunities your college offers for development.

23) **Apply for a grant.** Seek out on-campus or external grant sources related to improving classroom teaching and learning. Then, apply for a grant. Explore projects that involve collaboration between departments or disciplines.

24) **Don't worry.** Don't worry if some of what you are doing contradicts what you found in this list of ideas. Don't be too concerned if you discover your approaches are different from what your colleagues are doing. If it works, keep doing it. Check out Brookfield's "Fifteen Maxims of Skillful Teaching" in Appendix K. As Brookfield (2006) explains

> Listen to that inner, nagging voice that says you might be right and your superiors, your colleagues, your union, the professional code of conduct that you work under, and the writers of books like this one might be wrong. In a very real sense, you are the ultimate expert on your own experience so be ready to act on what this voice is telling you. And if you do act and find out that your hunch was wrong, you can remind yourself that continually making mistakes, and learning from these, is endemic to all good teaching. (p. 279)

25) **Make continuous self-appraisal, assessment, and reflection a habit.** There are many tools available for teachers to use to continually assess how they are doing as teachers; many were mentioned earlier in this book. Four reflection instruments have emerged from the results of The Engaged Teacher Survey; they are included as Appendices F, G, H, and I. Use them to spark meaningful discussions about teaching and learning on your campus.

Summary

I hope this chapter has influenced you to take the time to examine what you do as a teacher through discussion, observation, reflective appraisal, collaboration with other teachers, and professional growth opportunities. The goal was to illustrate what Bain stated in *What the Best College Teachers Do* (2004): "Part of being a good teacher (not all) is knowing that you always have something new to learn" (p. 174). If nothing else, I hope this chapter encouraged you to engage in reflective appraisal of your teaching approaches by including others. Keep on learning about how you help students learn.

Remember, what you do as a teacher is important work. How well you do it will benefit from frequent reflection, observation, analysis, revision, dialogue, and feedback.

Author Narrative: Marathon Teacher Stages

Teaching is a lot like running a marathon. On some training days, it's hard to show up and jog when I'm tired or sore or distracted, but I do. I might slow down, or adjust, but I keep on going. I am committed. I am passionate. I care. Just like the urge to keep on jogging, something inside of me drives me to teach. Teaching students is my passion. And, like running, it feeds my soul.

Most teachers experience several stages of growth and change throughout their careers. The stages are similar to those of a marathon runner. Throughout each stage, the role of our mentors changes and adjusts to our own growth, development, and needs.

In Stage One as teachers, we teach like we saw our mentors teach. We need to do this to master the fundamentals, tools, and techniques of teaching, and it's an essential period of indoctrination and growth as a teacher. We're clumsy at first, but if we truly care, we learn from our failings and improve. We rely on our mentors to guide us, inspire us, and boost us up with encouragement during this stage.

Next we move into Stage Two, where we teach from our own knowledge in our fields and our experiences as teachers. Soon, just like in a marathon, we've mastered the fundamentals and we're off, racing toward the classroom, where we do most of our work on our own. The starting gun goes off and we are moving along on our own, forging our own path, traversing over speed bumps and curves. We pick up speed and keep on going, until we have some sort of slow down, or breakdown of momentum. Until we arrive at the place where we realize that what got us to this place may keep us going, but the voice we hear is not our own. This is not a comfortable moment. It is scary for most of us. It may be the day a student pushes us over the edge. It may be the day we are tired and weary and spent. Or, it may simply be the day that we notice that students are no longer paying attention. But, if we pay attention to these telling signals we may begin to refine our own voice as we enter Stage Three of our teaching practice.

At this stage, we teach from who we are. It is when we truly begin to develop our voices as teachers, our own unique styles. In this stage, we discover that teaching is not merely a matter of technique or strategies. We learn that teaching is a matter of finding our own individual voice. If we accept this wake up call, and decide to go beyond technique, or what mentors did, or the advice of experts, we may enter into an insightful, reflective time of exhausting experimentation, from which our own true voices emerge. It is then that we know that all the teaching techniques and tools and tips are no substitute for who and what we are.

Students don't learn from our tools and techniques. They learn from us. We don't just teach classes, we teach students. Knowing our students, and knowing ourselves, is as important as knowing our subject matter.

Much like training for and completing a marathon, teaching requires a great deal of commitment, conditioning, and endurance. It is not a sprint, but a journey. It also requires the support of others—mentors, students, colleagues and college leaders—to navigate the journey. Just as running a marathon is more than merely strapping on some running shoes and jogging 26.2 miles, teaching is more than merely showing up for class. It is about setting goals and planning how to meet those goals and remaining flexible to changes in conditions along the way. It is about figuring out what areas need to be developed, what areas are weak and need more work, and what areas are neglected and need attention. The help of others keeps us on the teaching journey.

Teaching is also about figuring out what students need. What students fear. What stories, strengths and hopes they bring. We also should be aware that what happens in the classroom might not always be exactly what we planned to teach or how. The commitment required of a teacher cannot be conditional on the quality or ability of our students. It cannot be conditional on how we're treated by our institutions or departments. It comes from how we see ourselves and how we conduct ourselves as professionals executing teaching practices. Our commitment comes from who we are inside.

When we teach well and know students have learned well, everything in life just seems more hopeful and possible. Likewise, after running a marathon, everything in life just seems more possible.

Reflect and respond.

- What is your definition of engaged teaching and learning?
- How do you now use what the research has discovered about how people learn to drive your teaching practice? On the other hand, how often do you do something because your mentors or professors did it?
- What is the most important thing you've learned from reading The Engaged Teacher?
- How will you use what you've learned?

Engaged Teaching Strategy 9a: Teaching Timeline

Directions: Draw a timeline illustrating your history and your career stages as a teacher. Chronologically include the highlights, ups and downs, education, mentors, and significant experiences that you believe have influenced your teaching practice. Share and discuss with a colleague. This exercise can have a dramatic impact when used as a basis for discussion in a small group of faculty colleagues.

Expanded Engaged Teaching Strategy 9b: Teaching Circle "Stories"

Directions: Form a teaching circle of trusted colleagues and mentors for the purpose of sharing teaching stories. Be creative in defining how stories can be shared in writing, orally in discussion, as digital stories, etc. Broaden the scope of story topics to include experiences with students, as a learner, teaching, etc. Share and discuss. This activity can be facilitated formally as a professional development seminar on campus or informally as a group of teachers who occasionally meet to share stories.

Epilogue

Final Thoughts on Engaged Teaching

The growth of any craft depends on shared practice and honest dialogue among the people who do it. We grow by trial and error, to be sure — but our willingness to try, and fail, as individuals is severely limited when we are not supported by a community that encourages such risks.

— Parker Palmer

Engaged Teaching and Learning: No One Best Way

A life in teaching is a stitched-together affair, a crazy quilt of odd pieces and scrounged materials, equal parts invention and imposition. To make a life in teaching is largely to find your own way, to follow this or that thread, to work until your fingers ache, your mind feels as if it will unravel, and your eyes give out, and to make mistakes and then rework large pieces.

— William Ayers

The role of teachers has evolved to include different roles than in the past. Changes in the expectations for today's college teachers place new demands on teacher preparation and professional development. According to Mellow and Heelan (2008), instructional roles for today's teachers include the following: lecturer, expert, mentor, reflection facilitator, group discussion guide, intensive workshop leader, consultant, leader of intensive problem-based experiential learning, software developer or adapter of off-the-shelf software, and partner with co-curricular educators (p. 126).

Throughout these pages, I have attempted to convey the idea that it is possible for teachers to respond to changes in what they are expected to do while maintaining a focus on engaging students in meaningful learning experiences. Good teachers are not born good teachers. Good teaching can be learned. It is not just a matter of technique, but so much more.

Over the years, I have worked with numerous faculty and witnessed proof that by expanding their pedagogy to include many of the learner-centered ideas set forth in this book they did indeed engage students in significant learning. They better engaged students in learning by engaging themselves in learning more about teaching and learning. They became better teachers by applying research-based practices that help students learn.

There is not one "best" practice that emerged from The Engaged Teacher Study, but several that align with the literature and recent research on learning and effective teaching, including:

- Truly engaged teachers build rapport and engage with students in ways that value and empower them with the skills to persevere academically.
- Truly engaged teachers form student connections that are authentic, trustful, open, cooperative, and encourage student responsibility for learning.
- Truly engaged teachers are passionate about their subjects and teaching; they make learning relevant by developing active, learner-centered approaches to best connect with students' diverse knowledge, cultural, and learning backgrounds.
- Truly engaged teachers foster critical thinking and encourage students to become aware of how they are experiencing and applying learning; they teach students to know when they are learning.
- Truly engaged teachers know and bring themselves and their identities appropriately into their teaching practices to enhance their authenticity and credibility.
- Truly engaged teachers are connected with their inner, core beliefs and principles about students, subject, self and teaching/learning—and use both insights and scholarship to guide their practice.

As you continue to examine, revise, and refine your teaching practice, keep in mind that it should be constantly in flux. It is a process and product that reacts synergistically with the components of The Engaged Teaching Model: students, subject, self, and the scholarship of teaching and learning. Whenever you can, surround yourself with other teachers committed to continually seeking improvement by engaging today's students in significant and sustained learning.

In many ways, this book is a tribute to the scholar-practitioner teachers who passionately seek ways to engage students in learning, who are committed to teaching excellence, and who believe that they can make a difference in students' lives. I hope this book will inspire you to advance your passion for teaching and learning by continuously examining your own teaching practices.

References

Adelman, C. (2005). *Executive summary: moving into town—and moving on: The community college in the lives of traditional-age students.* Washington, DC: U.S. Department of Education.

Albom, M. (1987). *Tuesdays with Morrie: An old man, a young man, and life's greatest lesson.* New York, NY: Doubleday.

Alfred, R. L. (1994). Measuring teaching effectiveness. In T. O'Banion (Ed.), *Teaching and learning in the community college* (pp. 263-283). Washington, DC: Community College Press.

Ambrose, S. A., Bridges, M. W., DiPietro, M., Lovett, M. C., & Norman, M. K. (2010). *How learning works: Seven research-based principles for smart teaching.* San Francisco: Jossey-Bass.

American Association of Community Colleges. (2006). *Fast facts about community colleges.* Retrieved from http://www.aacc.nche.edu/ABOUTCC/Pages/fastfacts. aspx

American Council on Education. (1999). *To touch the future: Transforming the way teachers are taught. An action agenda for college and university professors.* Washington, DC: American Council on Education. Retrieved from http://www.acenet.edu/bookstore/pdf/teacher-ed-rpt.pdf

Angelo, T. A., & Cross, K. P. (1993). *Classroom assessment techniques* (2nd ed.). San Francisco: Jossey-Bass.

Bain, K. (2004). *What the best college teachers do.* Cambridge, MA: Harvard University Press.

Barkley, E. F. (2010). *Student engagement techniques: A handbook for college faculty.* San Francisco: Jossey-Bass.

Barr, R. B., & Tagg, J. (1995). From teaching to learning: A new paradigm for undergraduate education. *Change, 27*(6), 12-25.

Bloom, B. S. (1956). *Taxonomy of educational objectives: handbook I, cognitive domain.* New York: David McKay Company, Inc.

Boice, R. (1996). *First-order principles for college teachers: Ten basic ways to improve the teaching process.* Bolton, MA: Anker.

Brookfield, S. D. (2006). *The skillful teacher: On technique, trust, and responsiveness in the classroom* (2nd ed.). San Francisco: Jossey-Bass.

Buckingham, M., & Coffman, C. (1999). *First, break all the rules: What the world's greatest managers do differently*. NY: Gallup.

Chickering, A. W., & Gamson, Z. F. (1987). Seven principles for good practice in undergraduate education. *AAHE Bulletin, 39*(7), 3-7.

College Board. (2011). *Trends in college pricing: 2011*. Washington, DC: Author. Retrieved from http://trends.collegeboard.org/college_pricing/

Cooper, J. L., & Robinson, P. (Eds.). (2011). *Small group learning in higher education; Research and practice*. Stillwater, OK: New Forums Press.

Cox, M. D. (2004). *Faculty learning community program director's and facilitator's handbook*. Oxford, OH: Miami University.

Dewey, J. (1916). *Democracy and education: An introduction to the philosophy of education*. New York: Macmillian.

Filene, P. G. (2005). *The joy of teaching: A practical guide for new college instructors*. Chapel Hill, NC: University of North Carolina Press.

Fink, L.D. (2003). *Creating significant learning experiences: An integrated approach to designing college courses*. San Francisco, CA: Jossey-Bass.

Finkel, Donald L. (2000). *Teaching with your mouth shut*. Portsmouth, NH: Heinemann.

Fish, L. (1996). *The chalk dust collection: Thoughts and reflections on teaching in colleges & universities*. Stillwater, OK: New Forums Press.

Howe, N., & Strauss, W. (2000). *Millennials rising: The next great generation*. New York: Vintage Press.

Huston, T. (2009). *Teaching what you don't know*. Cambridge, MA: Harvard University Press.

Intrator, S. M. (2002). *Stories of the courage to teach: Honoring the teacher's heart*. San Francisco: Jossey-Bass.

Jensen, Eric. P. (2008). *Brain-based learning: The new paradigm of teaching*. Thousand Oaks, CA: Corwin Press.

Kane, T. J., & Rouse, C. E. (1999). The community college: Educating students at the margin between college and work. *Journal of Economic Perspective, 13*(1), 63-84.

Kolb, D. A. (1981). Learning styles and disciplinary differences. In A. Chickering (Ed.), *The modern American college* (pp. 232-255). San Francisco: Jossey-Bass.

Kuh, G., Kinzie, J., Schuh, J., Whitt, E., & Associates. (2005). *Student success in college: Creating conditions that matter*. San Francisco: Jossey-Bass.

Lamott, A. (1995). *Bird by bird: Some instructions on writing and life*. NY: Doubleday.

Lang, J. M. (2008). *On course: A week-by-week guide to your first semester of college teaching*. Cambridge, MA: Harvard University Press.

Light, R. J. (2001). *Making the most of college: Students speak their minds*. Cambridge, MA: Harvard University Press.

Luft, J., & Ingham, H. (1955). The Johari window, a graphic model of inter-personal awareness. *Proceedings of the western training laboratory in group development*. Los Angeles, CA: UCLA.

McKeachie, W. J. (1998). *Teaching tips: A guidebook for the beginning college teacher* (10th ed.). Lexington, MA: D.C. Heath.

McKeachie, W. J., & Svinicki, J. (2006). *Teaching tips: Strategies, research, and theory for college and university teachers* (12th ed.). Boston, MA: Houghton Mifflin.

Mellow, G. O., & Heelan, C. (2008). *Minding the dream: The process and practice of the American community college*. Lanham, MD: Rowman & Littlefield.

Millis, B. J., (2010). *Cooperative learning in higher education: Across the disciplines, across the academy*. Sterling, VA: Stylus.

National Center for Education Statistics. (2007a). *Integrated postsecondary education data system (IPEDS) completion survey* [Data file]. Washington, DC: U.S. Department of Education.

Nieto, S. (2003). *What keeps teachers going* (3rd ed.). New York: Teachers College Press.

Nye, B., Konstantopoulos, S., & Hedges, L.V. (2004). How large are teacher effects? *Educational Evaluation and Policy Analysis, 26,* 237-257.

Obama, B. (2009, July 14). Remarks by the president on the American Graduation Initiative. Washington, DC: The White House, Office of the Press Secretary. Retrieved from http://www.whitehouse.gov/the_press_office/Remarks-by-the-President-on-the-American-Graduation-Initiative-in-Warren-MI/

O'Banion, T., & Associates. (1994). *Teaching and learning in the community college*. Washington, DC: American Association of Community Colleges.

O'Banion, T. (1997). *A learning college for the 21st century*. Phoenix, AZ: Oryx Press.

Palmer, P. J. (1998). *The courage to teach: Exploring the inner landscape of a teacher's life*. San Francisco, CA: Jossey-Bass.

Parini, J. (2005). *The art of teaching*. New York: Oxford University Press.

Pew Research Center (2011). *Is college worth it? College presidents, public access, value, quality and mission of higher education*. May 16, 2011. Washington, DC: Pew Social & Demographic Trends. Retrieved from http://pewsocialtrends.org/2011/05/15/is-college-worth-it/

Phillipe, K. A. & Patton, M. (2000). *National profile of community colleges: Trends and statistics*. (3rd ed., pp 1-75). Washington, DC: Community College Press.

Povlacs, J. (1985). More than facts. *University of Minnesota (Duluth) Instructional Development, 4,*1-2.

Redmond, M., & Clark, D. (1982). Small group instructional diagnosis: A practical approach to improving teaching. *AAHE Bulletin.* 34(6), pp. 8-10.

Ridley, D. S., & Walther, B. (1995). *Creating responsible learners: The role of a positive classroom environment*. Washington, DC: American Psychological Association.

Rojek, D. G. (2001). Responsibilities of a college teacher. In F. J. Stephenson, *Extraordinary teachers: The essence of excellent teaching* (pp. 49-56). Kansas: Andrews McMeel Publishing.

Roueche, J. E., & Roueche, S. D. (1994). Creating the climate for teaching and learning. In T. O'Banion (Ed.), & Associates, *Teaching and learning in the community college* (pp. 21-40). Washington, DC: American Association of Community Colleges.

Roueche, J. E., Milliron, M. D., & Roueche, S. D. (2003). *Practical magic: On the front lines of teaching excellence*. Washington, DC: Community College Press.

Stephenson, F. (2001). *Extraordinary teachers: The essence of excellent teaching*. Kansas: Andrews McMeel Publishing.

Twenge, J. M. (2006). *Generation me: Why today's young Americans are more confident, assertive, entitled—and more miserable than ever before*. New York: Free Press.

Vaughn, G. B. (1994). The community college teacher as scholar. In T. O'Banion (Ed.), & Associates. *Teaching and learning in the community college* (pp. 161-178). Washington, DC: Community College Press.

Weimer, M. (1993). *Improving your classroom teaching*. Newburg Park, CA: Sage.

Weimer, M. (2002). *Learner-centered teaching: Five key changes to practice*. San Francisco: Jossey-Bass.

Appendix A

Essential Resources for Teaching and Learning

Ambrose, S. A., Bridges, M. W., DiPietro, M., Lovett, M. C., & Norman, M. K. (2010). *How learning works: Seven research-based principles for smart teaching.* San Francisco: Jossey-Bass.

Angelo, T. A., & Cross, K. P. (1993). *Classroom assessment techniques* (2nd ed.). San Francisco: Jossey-Bass.

Bain, K. (2004). *What the best college teachers do.* Cambridge, MA: Harvard University Press.

Barkley, E. F. (2010). *Student engagement techniques: A handbook for college faculty.* San Francisco: Jossey-Bass.

Boice, R. (1996). *First-order principles for college teachers: Ten basic ways to improve the teaching process.* Bolton, MA: Anker.

Bonwell, C. C., & Eison, J. A. (1999). *Active learning: Creating excitement in the classroom.* ASHE-ERIC Higher Education Report No. 1. Washington, DC: The George Washington University, School of Education and Human Development.

Brookfield, S. D. (2006). *The skillful teacher: On technique, trust, and responsiveness in the classroom* (2nd ed.). San Francisco: Jossey-Bass.

Chickering, A. W., & Gamson, Z. F. (1987). Seven principles for good practice in undergraduate education. *AAHE Bulletin, 39* (7), 3-7.

Cross, K. P., & Steadman, M. (1996). *Classroom research: Implementing the scholarship of teaching.* San Francisco: Jossey-Bass.

Davis, B. G. (2009). *Tools for teaching* (2nd ed.). San Francisco: Jossey-Bass.

Filene, P. G. (2005). *The joy of teaching. A practical guide for new college instructors.* Chapel Hill, NC: University of North Carolina Press.

Fink, L.D. (2003). *Creating significant learning experiences: An integrated approach to designing college courses.* San Francisco, CA: Jossey-Bass.

Gabriel, K. F. (2008). *Teaching unprepared students: Strategies for promoting success and retention in higher education.* Sterling, VA: Stylus.

Huston, T. (2009). *Teaching what you don't know.* Cambridge, MA: Harvard University Press.

Kuh, G., Kinzie, J., Schuh, J., Whitt, E., & Associates. (2005). *Student success in college: Creating conditions that matter.* San Francisco: Jossey-Bass.

Lang, J. M. (2008). *On course: A week-by-week guide to your first semester of college teaching.* Cambridge, MA: Harvard University Press.

McKeachie, W. J., & Svinicki, J. (2006). *Teaching tips: Strategies, research, and theory for college and university teachers* (12th ed.). Boston, MA: Houghton Mifflin.

Nilson, L. B. (2003). *Teaching at its best: A research-based resource for college instructors* (2nd ed.). Bolton, MA: Anker.

Palmer, P. J. (1998). *The courage to teach: Exploring the inner landscape of a teacher's life.* San Francisco, CA: Jossey-Bass.

Roueche, J. E., Milliron, M. D., & Roueche, S. D. (2003). *Practical magic: On the front lines of teaching excellence.* Washington, DC: Community College Press.

Tinto, V. (2011). *Taking student success seriously in the classroom.* Retrieved from http://www.league.org/publication/whitepapers/files/20110225.pdf.

Weimer, M. (2002). *Learner-centered teaching: Five key changes to practice.* San Francisco: Jossey-Bass.

Appendix B

Mid-Semester Assessment

Directions: Please do not put your name on this survey. I will use the feedback you provide to improve learning in this class. Please be as specific and concrete as possible with your opinions, thoughts, and suggestions. I will report back the feedback to you in the next 1-2 class meetings. Thank you very much.

1. What are the things in this class that help you learn?

2. What are the things *you* do to help yourself learn?

3. What specific ideas or suggestions do you have about this class? What would you like to see the instructor do?

4. Please describe the times in class when you've been most engaged; what were you doing?

5. Please describe the times in class when you've been least engaged; what were you doing? Describe times you've been puzzled or confused.

6. What are the strengths of the instructor and the course? What do you like that the instructor does? What do you find most affirming?

7. Is the pace of the course (circle one and explain below):
   Too fast   Too slow   Just right

(Adapted from Huston (2009) and Brookfield's (2006) Assessment Tools)

Appendix C

A Course-Based Guide for Academic Service-Learning: Questions for Faculty

A good place to start is to review the course design and syllabus, identify the learning objectives most suited to service-learning, and then ask: *"What is it my students could do in the community that relates to the objectives of this course and would enhance the academic value of my course?"* The faculty member *must* determine the best fit of service based on the learning objectives. The degree of importance of the competency may dictate the type or amount of service time required of the student, but the amount of time required is secondary to the *learning* that the faculty member seeks. Important questions and considerations include:

1. Considering the courses I teach, how could community service be helpful in enriching the discipline and helping students master the course objectives?

2. What kinds of course competencies might community service opportunities help students master or learn?

3. What are my goals in using the community service? (Link learning objectives to the community service and analyze how the service will reinforce, deepen and/or broaden the learning objective.)

4. What do I want my students to get from this experience?

5. How will the community benefit?

6. What kind of course service option is best?

7. What kinds of partnerships and projects are logical to link to the service-related objective? What types of community sites would be appropriate (nursing homes, homeless shelters, public schools, etc.)?

---

8. What specific service would such partnerships/projects provide to the larger community?

9. What is the best format for the service component (e.g., Honors Option, mandatory, extra credit, long term, short term, individual, group, one-time project, semester long project)?

10. What kinds of changes do I need to make to my course syllabus to reflect the change?

11. What kinds of adjustments should I make to the traditional workload for the course as a result of the service component (e.g., less reading, fewer tests, revised assignments)?

12. How many hours of service will I require? How will I keep track of student service hours?

13. What kinds of learning can the service component facilitate that are currently being covered/assessed in another way?

14. What kind of explanation will be included in the syllabus to let students know how the service component is related to the course content?

15. How will I prepare students for the community-based work? What kinds of strategies will help prepare students for their community-based work? (e.g., in-class orientation, training, presentation by agency, etc.)?

16. How can the community partner be of educational assistance?

17. What other strategies will prepare students—conceptually, personally, practically—for the community based work?

18. What kinds of learning agreements or contracts, if any, might be necessary for the community-based work?

19. What type of pre-assessment might be helpful at this point?

(A key question is "What are your fears, concerns, and/or expectations going into this service project?" This can be used in discussion, answered on note cards and collected, or used as the first entry in a reflection journal or log.)

20. What types of assessments, assignments, and reflection strategies will best help students link their service and classroom-based work? (e.g., journals, papers, presentations, etc.)?

Adding service-learning to a course requires clearly communicating to students the role of service in the course and how it connects to the course content. This will help them understand how what they are learning is directly applicable to their lives. The course syllabus should clearly define the precise role of service in achieving the course learning objectives and the nature of the service-learning assignment. Finally, the reflective or synthesis component of service-learning can tie together the why, what, and how so that both students and faculty can assess the impact of the service on learning. For examples of service-learning in higher education, Campus Compact is a comprehensive organization providing sample syllabi, assignments, training, and research.

Appendix D
Code of Ethical Classroom Conduct

Guidelines for Students:
- Please respect others/be courteous
- Interaction/whole class participation
- Constructive criticism/feedback
- Be specific
- Take time to get constructive criticism from others
- Good listening
- Respect each other's ideas and be open
- No side conversations while others are speaking
- Cell phone on vibrate/silence
- No hats while speaking in front of class
- No profanity, plagiarism, or sexist/racist/etc. remarks
- Participate regularly (see participation criteria in syllabus)
- Be a team player; don't slack
- Relate material to real world/work/education
- Stay on track/on time with assignments/group work
- Come to class prepared

Guidelines for Instructor:
- Speedy replies
- Relevant examples/relate stories to current topic
- Hands on activities
- Flexible meeting time/schedule
- Fun learning environment
- Informal attitude/climate
- Challenge and motivate students
- Technology
- Experience/funny/insightful
- Communication skills
- Enthusiastic, interactive, group activities/discussion, feedback

We hereby commit to following the guidelines we have created (please sign below):

Appendix E

Speech School Storytellers Service-Learning Assignment Feedback and Reflection Assessment

A. Rate YOURSELF: 5-excellent 4-good 3-average 2-fair 1-poor 0-absent

____On time, begin poised without rushing, give background (book, author, etc.)

____Gestures/movement   ____Facial expressions   ____Enthusiasm

____Avoided distracting mannerisms

____Used pauses effectively

____Grammar/pronunciation, articulated clearly

____Held interest of audience

____Used vocal variety to add impact (volume, pitch, rate, inflections, etc.)

____Contributed to Q & A/discussion   ____Props

____Q & A segment

B. When you first heard about the School Storyteller assignment, what were your thoughts, fears, expectations, and/or wishes?

C. How did today's experience match up with what you expected?

D. What were things that helped you learn and do well on this assignment?

E. What are some suggestions for improving your learning?

F. What is your reaction to the volunteer aspect of the assignment? Would you do it again?

G. What are the most important things you learned?

H. Give specific examples of how you applied course concepts and skills we are learning (audience analysis, vocal variety, etc.) as you executed this assignment.

I. What, if any, suggestions, questions, feedback, or thoughts do you have now?

Appendix F

The Engaged Student Questionnaire

Directions: Please do not write your name on this form. Your responses are intended to be anonymous and will not influence your grade for this course. Please answer honestly. Your responses will help me make changes to improve this course.

Please circle SA = Strongly agree, A = Agree, D = Disagree, SD = Strongly disagree, or N = Does not apply/do not know for each question. Please write out an explanation or example below each item to explain your response. Thank you!

1. I know what is expected of me in this class.
   SA A D SD N
2. I have the resources I need to do my best work in this class.
   SA A D SD N
3. I receive timely and helpful feedback from my instructor.
   SA A D SD N
4. When I do good work, I receive recognition for it in this class.
   SA A D SD N
5. My teacher seems to care about me and the other students.
   SA A D SD N
6. My opinions and feedback seem to count in this class.
   SA A D SD N
7. Most of the time, I feel engaged in learning in this class.
   SA A D SD N
8. I am given some choices about what and how I learn in this class.
   SA A D SD N
9. I am able to apply what I am learning in this class in relevant ways.
   SA A D SD N
10. Most of the time, I apply myself to do my best in this class.
    SA A D SD N

Please add any other comments or suggestions:

Appendix G

The Engaged Teacher Institutional Culture Questionnaire

Directions: Please do not write your name on this form. Your responses are intended to be anonymous (if used in a group, department, college-wide, etc.).

Please circle SA = Strongly agree, A = Agree, D = Disagree, SD = Strongly disagree, or N = Does not apply/do not know for each question. Please write out an explanation or example below each item to explain your response. Thank you!

1. I know what is expected of me as a teacher at this college.
   SA A D SD N
2. I have the resources I need to do my best work as a teacher.
   SA A D SD N
3. I receive timely and helpful feedback from my supervisor.
   SA A D SD N
4. When I do good work, I receive recognition and praise for it.
   SA A D SD N
5. My supervisor seems to care about me and the other teachers.
   SA A D SD N
6. My opinions and feedback seem to count at this college.
   SA A D SD N
7. Most of the time, I feel engaged as a faculty member.
   SA A D SD N
8. I am given choices about what and how I teach.
   SA A D SD N
9. I am supported to do my best work as a faculty member.
   SA A D SD N
10. Most of the time, I apply myself to do my best as a teacher.
    SA A D SD N

Please add any other comments or suggestions:

Appendix H

The Engaged Teacher Colleague/Supervisor Questionnaire

Directions: Please do not write your name on this form. Your responses are intended to be anonymous (if used in a group, department, college-wide, etc.).

Please circle SA = Strongly agree, A = Agree, D = Disagree, SD = Strongly disagree, or N = Does not apply/do not know for each question. Please write out an explanation or example below each item to explain your response. Thank you!

1. I know what is expected of me from my students.
   SA A D SD N
2. I have the resources I need to help students learn.
   SA A D SD N
3. I solicit feedback and suggestions from students and use it to improve learning in my classroom.
   SA A D SD N
4. When students do good work, I give recognition and praise for it.
   SA A D SD N
5. My students seem to care about the subject/learning.
   SA A D SD N
6. I seek the opinions and feedback of my students regularly.
   SA A D SD N
7. Most of the time, I keep my students engaged in active learning.
   SA A D SD N
8. I give students appropriate choices about what/how they learn.
   SA A D SD N
9. I support and challenge my students to do their best work.
   SA A D SD N
10. I regularly give feedback and discuss progress with students.
    SA A D SD N

Please add any other comments or suggestions:

Appendix I

The Engaged Teacher Self-Reflection Questionnaire

Directions: Please do not write your name on this form. Your responses are intended to be anonymous (if used in a group, department, college-wide, etc.).

Please circle SA = Strongly agree, A = Agree, D = Disagree, SD = Strongly disagree, or N = Does not apply/do not know for each question. Please write out an explanation or example below each item to explain your response. Thank you!

1. I use classroom assessment strategies to help understand how students learn.
   SA A D SD N
2. I am familiar with the literature on student learning and have access to the resources I need to help students learn.
   SA A D SD N
3. I solicit feedback and suggestions from colleagues and professionals and use it to improve learning in my classroom.
   SA A D SD N
4. When things aren't going well in my classroom, I seek help to understand why and make improvements.
   SA A D SD N
5. I care about the subject I teach, the students, and their learning.
   SA A D SD N
6. I seek the opinions and feedback of my students regularly.
   SA A D SD N
7. I regularly engage in professional development in my field.
   SA A D SD N
8. I regularly engage in professional development focused on the scholarship of teaching and learning.
   SA A D SD N
9. I challenge myself to do my best work and continually improve.
   SA A D SD N
10. I regularly seek feedback on how well my students are learning.
    SA A D SD N

Please add any other comments or suggestions:

Appendix J

Brookfield's "Fifteen Maxims of Skillful Teaching"

Maxim 1:   Expect Ambiguity
Maxim 2:   Perfection is an Illusion
Maxim 3:   Ground Your Teaching in How Your Students Are Learning
Maxim 4:   Be Wary of Standardized Models and Approaches
Maxim 5:   Regularly Reflect on Your Own Learning
Maxim 6:   Take Your Instincts Seriously
Maxim 7:   Create Diversity
Maxim 8:   Don't Be Afraid to Take Risks
Maxim 9:   Remember that Learning is Emotional
Maxim 10: Acknowledge Your Personality
Maxim 11: Don't Evaluate Yourself Only by Students' Satisfaction
Maxim 12: Remember the Importance of Both Support and Challenge
Maxim 13: Recognize and Accept Your Power
Maxim 14: View Yourself as a Helper of Learning
Maxim 15: Don't Trust What You've Just Read

(from *The Skillful Teacher: On Technique, Trust, and Responsiveness in the Classroom* (2nd ed.) by S. D. Brookfield, 2006)

Appendix K

Teaching Squares

Overview:
 Teaching Squares is a method of peer observation that will provide you with meaningful opportunities to observe your peers, analyze teaching approaches, apply new ideas in your own teaching practice, and celebrate good teaching! The goals of the Teaching Squares program are to help improve teaching skills and build community by using peer classroom observation and shared reflection (excluding judgment and evaluation). Faculty participants in a Square learn about the best practices of other faculty in order to improve their own teaching. Squares work best when paperwork is kept to a minimum. Suggested Observation Guide questions are included in this handout. Below is a suggested way to organize:

Week 1/Organize:
 Interested faculty meet as a group, form Squares and Square partners. Ground rules and observation times are set for the Squares (each person in a Square will be designated either A, B, C, or D). Review Ground Rules and see Observation Guide.

Ground Rules

 Each square can set its own ground rules; here are some to consider:
- What information is useful before the visit (syllabus, lesson plans, etc.)
- How long the visit should last
- The role of the visiting teacher
- How to schedule/give notice for classroom observations

Weeks 2, 3, 4/Observations (or every other week; your preference):
 Carry out visits; note observations and reflections (use Observation Guide). Your Square schedule might look like this:

Week 2: A visits B	B visits C	C visits D	D visits A
Week 3: A visits C	B visits D	C visits A	D visits B
Week 4: A visits D	B visits A	C visits B	D visits C

Week 5/Reflections:

Review your notes and share positive reflections with your Square partner. Note: You may want to schedule this time now; allow one hour.

Week 6/All Square Reflections:

All four Squares meet and review, share, discuss their experience and reflections. Use Review Session Guide. Schedule early to guarantee all four Squares are available for the final reflection session. Make it a celebration as well based on the wishes of the group. Debrief with a focus on what you've learned and how you're applying in *your* classroom to improve student learning. Remember, the focus of your Teaching Squares experience is *self-reflection,* not critique, evaluation, or advice giving.

Observation Guide (use one sheet for each visit)

During visit:
- Examples of good teaching and learning practices I observed
- What I have learned from observing this teacher
- What I might try as a result of this observation

After visit:
- What I tried since I visited my colleague
- What things worked well (student feedback details; assessment information)
- What I might do differently

Comments:
- What I liked and learned from this experience
- What things could be improved

Review Session Guide (for all Squares final review)

A. During your visits, what were things you observed that you might use to improve learning?

B. What things have you tried out, and what was the outcome (learning response, etc.)?
C. What did this experience teach you, or give you greater appreciation for, in terms of:
   - Your teaching colleagues
   - Your students
   - Specific aspects of teaching and learning
D. What are some of the things you liked about the Squares experience, and why?
E. What things could be improved?

Appendix L

Student Information Form

Welcome to (course name)! I look forward to working with you this semester, and need some basic information from you to better help me help you learn. Please fill out the information specified below and return this form to me before the end of class today. If you have any questions, please ask.

1. Name (please print):

2. Cell phone:

3. Emergency contact:

4. Major/program of study:

5. How many college credits have you completed?

6. Have you taken any other classes in this department? If so, please list.

7. What are your learning goals for this course? In other words, what would you like to know, gain, improve, or change by the end of this semester?

8. What problems, or issues, if any, do you anticipate?

9. What are your best strategies for succeeding in a college course?

10. What are your strengths as a learner?

11. What types of support from fellow students/the teacher help you do your best?

12. Is there any other information that would be helpful for me to know about you?

13. What questions, if any, do you have at this point?

Appendix M

Group Project Activity Log

Directions: Fill out the information below completely each time your group meets. Make sure you have contact information (cell phone numbers and email addresses) for each person in your group. Participation and follow-through is a major part of your grade for this project. **Return this completed sheet to your instructor.** Thank you.

Today's Date:

Group Name/Project:

Sign-in/role assignments for this meeting (please sign both first and last names; combine some roles if necessary):
    Leader:
    Recorder:
    Motivator:
    Task Master:
    Timer:
    Reporter:

Today's Tasks:

Today's Accomplishments:

To Do By When—By Who/Whom (identify dates and names below):

About The Author

Nancy Vader-McCormick, Ph.D., is a scholar, educator, and consultant with over 25 years as an innovative teacher. Her expertise includes engaging students through collaborative and active learning, academic service-learning, faculty development, and reflective practice.

Vader-McCormick currently serves as Coordinator of the Faculty Center for Teaching Excellence and as Professor in the Communication Department at Delta College. She is founder of the President's Speaker Series, founding Director of Academic Service-Learning, and the co-founder of the Student Food Pantry at Delta College. Her publications include *Academic Service-Learning: A Handbook for Faculty* and *Creativity: From the Inside Out.*

Vader-McCormick is the recipient of numerous honors, including the prestigious Bergstein Award for Teaching Excellence, the Scholarly Achievement Award, and the Don Laughner Award for Creative Change, all at Delta College. Other awards include the Innovation of the Year Award from the League for Innovation in the Community College, the University of Florida Institute of Higher Education Outstanding Graduate Award, and the Michigan Campus Compact Faculty and Staff Community Service-Learning Award.

Vader-McCormick earned a doctorate in administration in higher education from the University of Florida, two master's degrees from Central Michigan University, and a BS from Western Michigan University. She has worked in higher education for nearly three decades, starting in student services and moving to academics. In addition to teaching at Delta College for nearly 20 years, she has also taught at Central Michigan University and Saginaw Valley State University. Vader-McCormick has developed training programs for business and industry, provided keynote conference presentations and sessions, and consulted for higher education entities.

Index